THE GROCER'S BOY

ROBERT MURRAY

THE GROCER'S BOY

A Slice of His Life
in 1950s Scotland

Robert Murray

The Grocer's Boy: A Slice of His Life in 1950s Scotland by Robert Murray.

First published in Great Britain in 2018 by Extremis Publishing Ltd.,
Suite 218, Castle House, 1 Baker Street, Stirling, FK8 1AL, United Kingdom.
www.extremispublishing.com

Extremis Publishing is a Private Limited Company registered in Scotland (SC509983) whose Registered Office is Suite 218, Castle House, 1 Baker Street, Stirling, FK8 1AL, United Kingdom.

A CIP catalogue record for this book is available from the British Library.

ISBN: 978-0-9955897-2-8

Typeset in Goudy Bookletter 1911, designed by The League of Moveable Type.

Printed and bound in Great Britain by IngramSpark, Chapter House, Pitfield, Kiln Farm, Milton Keynes, MK11 3LW, United Kingdom.

MAP OF THE
COUNTY OF ANGUS

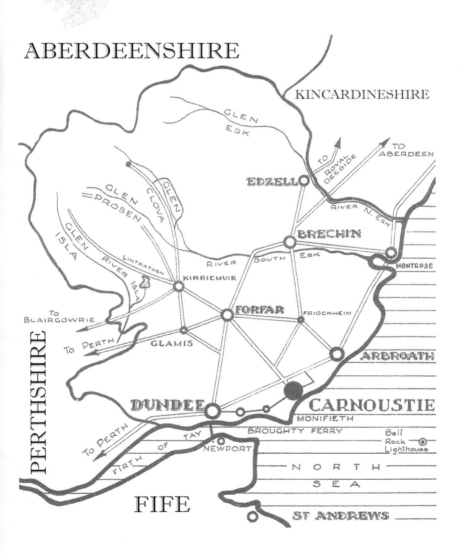

STREET MAP OF THE BURGH OF

CARNOUSTIE, CIRCA 1950s

KEY

1) Annfield Cottage
2) Wm. Low & Co. Ltd.
3) Police Station
4) Anchor Place
5) The Ballaster
6) Scout Hut
7) Post Office (GPO)
8) "South America" Cottages
9) London/Aberdeen Railway
10) Farm Bothy
11) Newton Panbride Church

Dedicated to Mum and Dad for their loving care and guidance, and in fond memory of Isobel.

With love to my daughters Carys and Wendy and grandchildren Lucy, Jonny, Charlie and Alfie.

"Never under estimate the power and value of your upbringing; strive to be best at whatever you do."

And love to my brother Peem and wee sister, "Baby Jean".

Carnoustie High Street in the 1950s

THE GROCER'S BOY

A Slice of His Life
in 1950s Scotland

Robert Murray

CHAPTER 1

How It All Started, or "Jings, Crivvens! An Interview!"

June 1953

SITTING on the doorstep of the senior pupil's entrance at Carnoustie school playground, I felt the warm June sun on my back. The substantial grey stone building had been constructed in the early 1900s, and I could still see scars on the school boundary wall where the Second World War air-raid shelters had been built but subsequently demolished. I remembered the dusty days, about three years previously, when the bulldozers had done their work.

With a damaged straw I was trying to suck up the dregs in my bottle of free milk and worrying about my mum's illness when Jim rushed up to me.

"Hey, Robbie! Do you want a job?"

"What kind o' job?"

"Well, ye ken I deliver butchery meat for the Co-op and this is my big year to lave the skale? So ye can ha'e my job if you want."

"What's the 'oors?"

"Fower tae six every nicht, and a' day Seturdays. Nothin' on Tuesdays, 'cos that's half day."

"What's the job, Jim?"

"Easy. Just deliverin' meat: sometimes jars o' potted hough. Nothin' heavy."

"Would I need to work in the shop?"

"Just sweep the flair and pit doon new sa'dust."

"Do I need tae cut meat or use the mincer?"

My mum had told me a young butcher had recently lost an arm in the big electric Co-op mincing machine, so I was cautious.

"No nothin' like that."

"And the pay?"

"Seven shillin's and sixpence a week, an' a pound o' mince."

This seemed a great chance – 37.5p, and mum would make good use of the mince too. She would probably use it to make her Sunday mince pie.

"Jings, that's nearly double the money I get for carryin' Christie's heavy bag o' papers on dark icy mornins, six days a week."

"Whit dae ye think then, Robbie?"

"Mum'll no' be happy, Jim. She'd worry aboot me and the mincer. I'll try to persuade her, but I'm sure she'll say no. Anyway, I'm really worried aboot her. I think she's seriously ill, 'cos she's gettin' awfi fat."

"Gee whiz, Robbie. Maybe she's 'preggars'."

"What does that mean? Is that a serious disease?"

"Dinna be daft! She could be expectin' a bairn."

"No, no, Jim. That canna be. I'll never believe that!"

"Well, forget aboot your mum. You'll need to hurry, 'cos Johnny Ross is desperate to get my job. If you dinna come back tae me by the end o' next week, I'll need tae gie it tae him. My boss keeps askin' if I've found somebody tae tak ow-er fae me."

Jim lived near me at Westhaven (the Ha'en), a fishing village at the east end of Carnoustie. He was a tall, muscular fifteen year old, and had been allowed to wear long breeks for years. I was only twelve and still in shorts. I'd been trying to persuade mum to buy me 'longers', but she kept saying she couldn't afford them. Some pals in my class already wore long trousers, and I wanted to look grown up too because I always thought the girls in my class giggled about boys in shorts. Mum may relent if I earned more money.

Jim had always been a helpful pal, and had taught me how to fish off the rocks. I'd helped him to look after fisher-man's boats at the harbour, and I knew he was looking after my best interests. Although I wanted the job, I found it im-possible to pluck up the courage to ask mum. Days passed, and the dilemma grew in my mind. Was Johnny Ross going to beat me to it? I now had two worries: not just about her fat-ness, but whether I should mention the Co-op job.

"What's wrong with you, Robert? You've done noth-ing but sit and listen to that radio all week. You're not your-self," mum said one day. "Are you feeling alright?"

"I'm fine, mum. I just enjoy listening to the radio now-adays," I lied.

Mum and dad had a Vidor radio which worked off a dry battery, as opposed to the bottles of acid that could be recharged. We had some favourite programmes we regularly listened to. On Saturday evenings there was the The MacFlannels' kitchen comedy *Down at the Mains*, and two or three times a week we tuned into *The Ovaltineys* which was so popular we wrote letters to the programme-makers and joined the Ovaltiney Club. This secured us a letter, a badge, and the words of the show's song: "We Are Ovaltineys, Little Girls and Boys". Sometimes, if we had no school next day, there was *Dick Barton: Special Agent* – a detective series which came on about 9.15 pm – but mum was not happy for us to listen to that.

On Sundays there was a programme which presented the popular songs of the week – an early version of *Top of the Pops*. I listened as often as I was allowed to, as I liked to whistle the top tunes as I cycled to and from school. While I waited for the answer about my Co-op job, the top songs seemed relevant to my plight. One was *I Believe* by Frankie Laine, and becoming more popular was *Answer Me*, sung by David Whitfield. I wasn't sure if I liked them, but the words were appropriate.

It was a Tuesday and I was whistling the tune to *Answer Me* when, out of the blue – just a day before Jim's deadline – he called to me as I cycled into the playground. I remember hoping he wouldn't give me a last chance offer, because I'd have to decline. Johnny Ross would get the job, and I'd miss out on a great opportunity.

"Robbie! Do you ken Freddie Smith?"

I knew him by sight, because he was a pal of his cousin who was in my class. He always seemed friendly, but I didn't know him.

"Well, he's asked me if I ken onybody to tak ower his job at Willie Low's the grocers. He laves skale at the same time as me. It's a better job than mine. I telt him you micht like it."

"What will the job be?"

"Deliverin' groceries. Heavy boxes, but you get a bike wi' a big basket. Same 'oors, but thirteen and six a week plus tips."

Jings! 67.5p! That solved the problem of telling mum. There were several High Street grocers in the town – some sold wines and spirits like the high class shop where my school pal Jock worked. But Willie Low's was a bigger, brighter and busier-looking shop than any of them, and it was on my way home from school.

"Okay. Tell Freddie I'll tak it."

"Thank goodness! Johnny Ross will get my job after all."

I cycled home as fast as I could to tell mum, who was tidying up the wash house when I rushed in.

"Mum! I've got a job! Message laddie with Willie Low's. Thirteen and six a week, plus tips! But I won't be home for tea till after six," I said, gasping for breath.

"My goodness! That's a lot of money. But it's an awful big bike, is it not? Do you think you'd manage?"

"Oh, yes!"

"Do you really want to do a job like that? There'll be a lot of heavy lifting. I think you should ask dad first."

"No, honestly, mum. I know I could do it," I impatiently argued, being disappointed by her reaction.

"Well, alright then. If you're sure you'll manage. Dad's on late shift, but I'll speak with him when he comes home tonight. He might not think it's good for you."

"I wish I could get a job like that!" said my brother Peem, who was a year younger than me but – for his age –

was stronger and more athletic. 'Peem' is a diminutive form for the name 'James', popular in the north-east of Scotland; from the 1930s to the late '50s, a mischievous young laddie called 'Wee Peem' appeared as a character in D.C. Thomson's comic *The Beano* and later their magazine *The People's Journal.*

I found it difficult to sleep that night, and I silently prayed that dad wouldn't stop me. But in the morning, he said it was alright so long as I was careful on the big bike. I hadn't seen Freddie for ages, but one day he hailed me in the playground.

"Meet me at the shop the morn at 4 o'clock. The boss wants to see you."

"Okay, Freddie."

Jings, crivens! An interview? What would I say? In my mind, I already had the job. I'd told Mr Christie I was leaving at the end of the week. I felt bad about that, as I'd been delivering his papers for nearly two years and he was a good boss with summer time car trips for Peem, me, and his other paperboy who was a girl called Norma. On our first trip, he and his wife took us to the dangerous hairpin bend on the Braemar road known as Devil's Elbow, and the next year to Pitlochry Hydro Dam when, on the way, they treated us to strawberries and ice cream at the Garden Tearoom at Dunkeld. What would happen if the boss didn't like me? How stupid had I been? Mr Christie had always been a kind boss, and I'd have to apologise and ask for my job back. I could tell he was disappointed with me when I said I was leaving.

I remember the evening mum told Peem and me that when she paid for the weekly newspaper, Mr Christie the newsagent in the High Street had asked her if the boys would like paperboy jobs: a large round in the Carlogie Road area, and a small one around Westhaven. My immediate reaction was yes, and Peem added that he'd like to do the smaller round.

It meant getting out of bed at 6.30am every morning except Sundays, and arriving in the shop at 7.00am. Our rounds were complete by 8 o'clock, which gave us time to have breakfast, change our clothing, and set off to school. My pay was four shillings a week. Not much, but it helped to buy little extras. There were some wet and windy days accompanied by dangerous dogs, but it was a joy on bright sunny mornings when the birds were singing to get out and see the world. (There was also a chance to read the news headlines as I delivered.) On cold, dark mornings mum would get on her own bike and help both Peem and me so that we could finish early.

* * *

Freddie was at the front door when I arrived for my interview. I'd never been in the premises, and it was strange to be taken to the back shop as it was like entering a secret place where assistants were going about their work. A strange mixture of food smells filled the air – fruity, spicy and cheesy.

Freddie introduced me to the boss, Mr Stewart, who looked quite severe and a bit twitchy. He kept hopping from one foot to another. He wore a clean white shop coat with white buttons. His sleeves were rolled up, and he had a blue shirt with a starched collar and a patterned tie. He was a lean man with a pale face and big staring eyes, and his brown hair parted in the centre was generously Brylcreemed. Although he looked serious, I detected a friendly glint in his eyes.

"Right then, Robert; let's go to the back shop. Freddie, just get on with your work."

The boss zoomed off. He walked so quickly, I had to run to keep up with him. He sat on a wooden crate then, indicating an unopened box of South African oranges, said: "Right, sit you down there. So you're the well-behaved, hard-working skinny redhead I've been told about."

I didn't like the skinny comment, but it was true. Then he fired questions at me.

"What's your full name?"

"Robert Taylor Murray."

"Alright, Robert. Do you know what the job is all about?"

"Aye. Delivering groceries."

"Well, it's more than that. You must help with jobs around the shop. Can you lift heavy boxes?"

"I lift big boxes for the fishermen."

"Are you healthy?"

"Aye, I'm never aff skale. Oh, but I was once aff for two days wi' liver fluke that I picked up at a Scout camp."

"Can you ride a bike?"

"Aye. I've had a bike since I was ten."

"Do you know the streets of Carnoustie?"

"Aye, I ken a lot of streets 'cos I've had a paper roond."

"You mean 'yes' not 'aye', 'know' not 'ken', and 'round' not 'roond'. You have to speak properly now, you know. No more 'affs' or *you'll* be off."

"Sorry."

"Are you a good timekeeper?"

"I've only been late for school once, when I had a puncture."

"Right, then. Your pay will be thirteen shillings and sixpence a week, paid to you each Saturday. You need to be here no later than five minutes past four every night, and 8.30 on Saturday mornings. Remember, talk nicely to my customers; no more 'ayes' and 'kens' and 'roonds'. Look after the message bike. If you have any problems, tell me and then Clark's bike shop will deal with any repairs. I don't like wasting money on batteries, so switch off when not on the road. Do you understand all that?"

"Aye. I mean, yes. Sorry."

"Any questions?"

"When do I finish, Mr Stewart?"

"You finish when your deliveries are done, and everything is put away. Anything else?"

"Yes. I didn't know I'd have a job, and I'm booked to go to a Scout camp for a week in July. Can I still do that?

"Well, yes, but you'll need to find somebody to stand in for you. Remind me the week before you go. Is that it?"

"So you're the wee skinny redhead?"

"Yes, thank you."

"Right then, Robert. Go around with Freddie during his last week. He'll show you the ropes. No pay while you train."

In an instant, he dashed back in the direction of the front shop. As he went, he was chanting: "Go, go, greasy grocer go!" I followed to meet up with Freddie.

Gee whiz, that was it. I did have the job. My mind was spinning and I felt like I'd just come out of a classroom after a difficult exam, but I couldn't wait to tell mum and dad that I'd had a tough interview and got the job. More than that, I wanted to be out on the road on the message bike.

As I cycled over the railway crossing on my way home, I suddenly remembered that I hadn't told Mrs Miller – who ran The Bookstall – that I was going to leave my Saturday evening job with her. So I did an about-turn on my bike and spoke to her.

"I'm sorry, Mrs Miller. I've got a job with Willie Lows delivering groceries at thirteen shillings and sixpence a week, and I won't be able to do your delivery now."

"On you go, son. It's good money for you, and you've done a grand job for me," she said while I sat on my bike and leaned against the edge of her counter. That was typical of Mrs Miller's helpful, business-like attitude.

I'd been delivering the Saturday *Sporting Post* to her newspaper shop since I was nine, and always received a threepenny piece (1.5p) for the first year or so. Then Mrs Miller started to give me a packet of Spangles sweeties as an extra. The shop has long since gone, but the recess in the wall of the stationmaster's house where the wooden structure fitted is still clearly seen today.

As I lay in bed that night, I couldn't help thinking about the unexpected events of June 1953 because so much had happened. My school pal Alan Craigie had invited me to watch the Queen's Coronation on television at his house. He was a close school pal, lean and wiry with red hair and more technically-minded than myself. I'll never forget walking out of the sunlight and entering a darkened room in his mum and dad's flat. The curtains were closed, and the room was packed full of people all watching a tiny black and white screen about the size of my school jotter page. There was an anguished 'sssshhussshh' whenever anyone was silly enough to speak over Richard Dimbleby's informed commentary.

The Coronation made me think seriously about my Scout Promise and how I wouldn't be saying 'to obey the Scout law and honour the King'. It would now be 'the Queen', and that seemed strange. It didn't seem right to me that a woman would be expected to rule, especially if we had another war. The way I looked at it then, Kings sounded stronger than Queens.

Later, I started to imagine the danger and freezing conditions that Hillary and Tensing must have endured when climbing Mount Everest. I'd seen film on Pathé News at the picture house – what a feat!

My concerns about mum's fat tummy had taken over my thoughts again. Was she ill? I had tried to work out what was wrong with her, but my own big news filled my mind – I would be a message laddie with Willie Low's! My excitement was tempered by only one question. Had my unbroken glorious summer days of fishing off the rocks and looking after boats at Westhaven ended? I had enjoyed what I considered to be a near miracle when the family moved to the Ha'en from a tiny cottage. My mind drifted over all the events which had brought me to my adventure playground.

I had lived at Anchor Place, Admiral Street, Westhaven since 1946 when I was five. Born in a bungalow in Barry – a small village west of Carnoustie – in October 1940, my family moved to Annfield Cottage at Barry Road in the town when I was two years old. I commenced school at Barry, half a mile away, in August 1945 when I was four. Mum and dad moved to Westhaven in February 1946 and until July that year mum, to keep me in a stable school environment, each day put me on a bus at Carlogie Road at the east end of the town, asking the conductress to make sure I got off nearly two miles later at Barry School. I recall every nervous moment of those early journeys, most especially the return trip when I had to board the bus and explain where I had to get off. Those travels ended when that school year finished, and I started school at Carnoustie in August 1946.

The house at Westhaven was an upstairs flat in a substantial stone-built block with a separate communal washhouse. The living accommodation consisted of two bedrooms and a living room, and was bigger and brighter than the Annfield Cottage. It also boasted a family toilet on the indoor landing. Gas lighting was a more welcome aspect compared to the paraffin lamps in Annfield. Although gas was easier than paraffin, Dad had a strict rule. When arriving home, we all had to stand still on the landing while he unlocked the front door. If he couldn't smell gas, he lit a match and then walked the length of the living room to the gas light fitting above the mantelpiece. We could hear the distinctive soft 'flop' as the gas flame lit the mantle. Only when the gauze fabric was bright yellow were we allowed to walk into the living room.

"Never walk into a dark house – it's too dangerous," he always told us.

It was at Westhaven that Peem and I made new friends. One was Billy (nicknamed Coffie, as his surname was Coffin), who was in Peem's class at school and was equally muscular and always had ideas for making things and inventing games. The other was Ollie, who was two years their junior and a gentle, timid boy. And of course there was Jim with the longers. We lived a hundred yards from the main London-Aberdeen railway line, and about the same distance from the narrow valley-shaped grassy ballaster. This was our playground, which extended almost the length of a football pitch and occupied space between the end of Admiral Street and the patches of maram grass covering sand dunes at the top of the beach. Ollie's dad, who was a coastguard, had told him it was so called because sand had been dug out over many years to provide ballast for boats.

"I can see the sea from our bedroom," I remember excitedly calling out to mum and dad on our arrival.

I had said goodbye to Miss Bell, my caring and motherly teacher, and ended my nerve-wracking bus trips to Barry school. Then my first school summer holiday started, and day by day the new world of Westhaven was gradually and gently revealed. Everything was new, and it was a time of exploration and discovery – the start of my formative years which, to this day, I can't imagine a life without such richness. When dad was working on shifts, mum took us for walks along the beach where we played in the sand and explored the small rock pools. Sometimes we walked to Carnoustie bay, paddled in the cool salty water, and had a picnic – which mum called our 'shivery bite'.

The Ha'en was our personal oyster which seemed to have been created only for us, and the pearl was another joy which came later in the summer: the harbour. There was no jetty or sea-wall or enclosed harbour. Boats were moored all summer in orderly fashion between two rows of rocks. The bow warp was attached to a long rock formation, and the stern rope was fixed to another nearer the shore. There was some protection from rough seas, but not a lot. Long poles were embedded into the highest rocks surrounding the harbour so that fishermen could follow a safe passage.

Westhaven was a wonderful world. The salty aroma of the sea and the ever-present – if less pleasant – smell of decaying seaweed added to the mix of sunshine and the breezes. We watched cormorants drying wings while perched on harbour poles. Now and again flocks of screeching oyster catchers would fly in formation, rising and dipping above the undulating rocks. As we waded through shallow pools and across the sandy channel of the harbour, we saw the gentle movement of the slowly advancing tide rising and picking up dry sand as it trickled its way through narrow channels in the rocks.

Leerie the lamplighter came around our streets and ignited the gas street lamps, and during daytimes a bread van man dispensed half or full loaves, having used a long-handled 'paddle' to pull them to the back of his van. Another door to door delivery was milk, which was delivered in pint size bottles by lads who jumped on and off a platform attached to the rear of the open-topped lorry.

It was my magical world; a boy's dream where we fished, sailed boats, played football and cricket, had our Hallowe'en bonfires, and did naughty things like smoking Woodbine cigarettes under the upturned boats in winter and chased by the local Bobby for burning dead marram grass in spring. I had found a complete new world. So now it was 1953 and change was in the air. My mind was in a whirl as I looked back over the years, and I sensed a chapter may be at an end.

Worries about mum kept recurring and, much as I tried, they wouldn't go away. My brain was swamped about something I thought would never happen. A baby would have a devastating effect on me and my family; I feared something which seemed catastrophic. My first inkling of a problem was during one teatime in June when we were all, except dad, sitting around the table. Mum was pouring tea into cups. She wasn't wearing her usual apron or 'pinnie' that day, but a colourful garment like a lightweight coat. As she stood at the table I thought mum looked fatter than usual. I never asked any questions and didn't even speak with Peem about my observation. From that day on I watched. Was she expecting a baby like Jim had said? If mum and dad were concerned about where every penny came from, how could they afford a baby? I couldn't make up my mind if it was happening or not. If it was a baby, I remember being embarrassed about it. What would my pals say? I was nearly thirteen and nobody I knew had a baby brother or sister.

Something told me I had to look forward. Next week would be the start of a new chapter in my life – a discovery of a different kind. Where would it lead?

CHAPTER 2

A Nervous Start, or "I've No Change Today, Son"

June 1953

THE Sunday prior to my training week with Freddie was a warm, sunny day. The start of my message bike job would, I thought, have a serious impact on my carefree life at the Ha'en. I was feeling slightly confused and disappointed at my impending loss, and I went to sit in my favourite place in the long grass at the ballaster – a place I sometimes frequented when there was something to mull over. Gentle scent from the many wild flowers around me wafted in the air while crickets or grasshoppers continuously chirped. The tide was well out, and the ozone smell of the sea and the seaweed was powerful. I saw the familiar named rocks Poddlie, Limpy and Dargie, but there was nobody out fishing. Why was I not there? What a waste! With nobody else about I had the whole place to myself, and I started turning over everything in my mind. Mum was my greatest concern. Was she ill? Would she die? None of my pals had a mother that was fat like mum, and I realised my powerlessness and embarrassment. My job: would it really change my freedom? Then I recalled that Jim, in our early days of fishing, had never missed a tide to fish with us – but in the last year or so he had, because of his Co-op job. What would happen to Peem and Coffie and Ollie? They would be left on their own, and their world would change too. Just then, a Meteor jet flew so low from west to east along the line of the beach that I could clearly see the pilot. It was followed by a Vampire jet. Each time we'd seen those planes while we played, they'd been part of our freedom. Part of our boys' side-show entertainment treat. Our carefree world of the rocks and fishing was real, but now jets seemed different. They represented the real harsh world of wars, and now I was facing the prospect of a real world too. Was my super sunshine sphere, where it never seemed to rain, beginning to tarnish?

My gaze took me to the grassy hollow where, in seemingly endless summer evenings, we'd played rounders and cricket. Mums and dads had joined in. I closed my eyes and I could picture the scene and hear the laughter. All the oohs and aahs, and the applause when somebody scored a run. How Donald Ford – aged about eight or nine – could bowl everyone out, even the dads, but no one could ever remove him from the stump. And now he was gone too. No longer did he come to holiday at the Ha'en as he had for years. Donald went on to play cricket and football for Scotland. We all knew then he was a genius with a ball, and I look back and think how privileged we were to play against or alongside him. Was my boyhood bubble bursting?

I wasn't reminiscing only about the evenings at the ballaster. My whole Westhaven experience was in my thoughts.

The glorious days of fishing and boating with Jim, Ollie falling in the sea, and the porpoises and dolphins. The exciting moments of guising, fireworks at the bonfire, and playing cheeky chicki-melli. The drama of the Coastguard shipwreck practice. The side-show of trainspotting. My walks home from the Scouts. All of it was etched in my memory. Westhaven wasn't just an address; it was a world, a globe – a glorious wonderland of life, fun and excitement where we never saw trouble or unhappiness. We didn't recognise the poverty we had, because our lives were so rich. Yes, things were changing. Would my fishing days end?

* * *

During the early part of my first week I pedalled around town with Freddie. From Wednesday onwards, I was allowed to ride the message bike and Freddie coasted along on his. All I had to remember were the customers' locations. If the customer had paid cash, there would be a rough slip of paper showing name and address with the order. Otherwise there would be full details on a handwritten invoice. The shop staff would tell me the sequence in which orders had to be delivered, and Freddie had said the pattern of deliveries was nearly the same each week.

The bike, in good condition, was painted black and specially made for the job. Unlike bicycles today it had no gears, but it did have mudguards! The rear wheel was like that of an ordinary bike, but the front wheel was much smaller, leaving room above it for a big metal frame containing a wicker basket in which the cardboard boxes were placed. Within the main triangular frame was a metal plate with 'Wm Low & Co. Ltd' painted in bold white letters. I remember thinking I'd have to behave myself, because people would know where to complain. When full of boxes, the bike was top-heavy and difficult to steer, and I recalled my science teacher's words about the centre of gravity. With the weight of goods on the front wheel it was liable to tip forward should the small wheel hit even any minor obstruction.

"Now, Robbie; you need to know how to pack boxes in your basket," said Freddie. "The first thing you need to realise is that the maximum you can carry inside the basket is either two big boxes, one on top of the other, or two smaller boxes on top of another two. The best small boxes to use are Heinz soup or baked beans ones. Whether you use large or small boxes, you need to put these strips of wood across the top of the bottom boxes. That stops any damage to goods below." Freddie used empty boxes to demonstrate, and showed me how to position the wood strips.

"That's it. Now all you need to do is cover everything up." As he said that, he placed a clean jute sack over the top of the boxes. "Keep the sack clean. Oh, and always get your boxes back; they can be scarce. Keep tyres hard, and remember you've got a wee wheel on the front so don't try to pedal up pavements or you'll cowp. In winter, use your bike lights sparingly. The boss hates spending money on batteries."

This was my chance to ask Freddie about some things that puzzled me.

"Why does the boss move like lightning all the time?"

"Don't know. He's been like that since I knew him. Maybe it's the way grocers move."

"And why does he keep repeating 'Go, go, greasy grocer go' all the time?"

"It's just the way he is. He's always rushing around saying that. Don't worry about it. Oh, and by the way, remember: when you get a tip, always take it as a pleasant surprise. Don't expect a tip, and don't accept it as if you earned it. Customers like to think they have been nice to you. My mum told me that, and it works."

"Thanks, Freddie."

The bike was fitted with a stand. Freddie showed me how to kick it down, then pull the bike back so that it stood upright on its own. He explained that it was crucial to park on a level surface. I listened intently to everything Freddie told me, and I was pleasantly surprised when Freddie said he had to lower the seat a few inches as I would otherwise have encountered a problem with it being set too high. With the use of a spanner Freddie dealt with that, and I was ready for the road. As I cruised up to the front door of the shop, I enjoyed finding the knack of kicking down the stand at exactly the right moment as I glided to a halt. By Saturday I'd learned the customer's addresses and how to pack boxes into the wicker basket, and Freddie's last words to me were "All the best next week, Robbie! Go, go, greasy grocer go!" as he laughed loudly.

On Monday there was only one delivery. It was to Miss Barrie, *The Willows*: three pounds of plain flour and two nutmegs.

"I've never seen Miss Barrie. I was told don't ring the bell, just leave the box in the outside larder." Freddie's words came to mind. What puzzled me was why Freddie had never seen this customer.

The house was a huge, white, prominent Victorian looking building in a very commanding position overlooking the town. It seemed massive for what I imagined was one old lady.

A large walled garden encircled the property, and a long winding path led to the front door and a side path to the back of the house where the separate stone built larder stood, the interior walls of which were entirely white-washed.

The interior air was cold and damp and, as directed, I left the box on a thick scrubbed stone shelf beside a large porcelain sink. As I walked back to the front gate, I wondered what Miss Barrie did with the flour and nutmegs every week.

My English teacher had told us the population of Carnoustie was around five thousand, and I started to wonder how many people would eat food that I'd deliver. I began to feel I was now an active part of the town, which was linear in shape running east-west and parallel to the coastline. There were many large private properties at the eastern end, while council houses dominated in the west. Where would most of my cycling be?

My first delivery done safely, I remember thinking I was now officially the Willie Low message laddie. With no other deliveries, I wondered what other jobs would be given to me. I'd learned the previous week the names of the staff, but I wasn't sure who would give me my duties. Both questions were answered as soon as I returned, when Mr Stewart dashed past me saying: "Tell Cathie you're ready for your tour."

In addition to the boss, there were three ladies on the staff. I'd already heard their names. Cathie was plump, had black hair, and looked the oldest. She appeared efficient, friendly and business-like, and seemed to know everything that went on. I got the impression that she could have been a school teacher, and guessed she'd been there a long time – maybe even longer than Mr Stewart. Isobel was possibly the youngest, as I'd gathered she'd left school in 1950. She was a very cheery, giggly and likeable person, and was quite stout. Both Cathie and Isobel lived somewhere in the country, because I'd heard them mention getting an early bus home. Dot was quiet, small and thin, with a large nose. I think she was the only married lady. One day she told me her grown-up son was about my age, yet she didn't look as old as Cathie or my mum.

Cathie took me to the counter area which I'd walked through during the previous week and, as we faced the windows, she explained: "This is called the front shop. On the left side we have fruit, sweets and biscuit displays, and on the other we sell provisions. That's bacon, cooked meats and dairy goods. We serve customers only from the provisions side, and that's where the only till is."

The front shop looked about the size of half a tennis court. It had two long counters running at right angles to the windows, and I could see there was a long marble top counter on the provisions side. The shop was very well-lit, with six large white electric lampshades spherical in shape hanging on chains in two rows.

"Now, behind the front shop there are three separate parts. The back shop where we are now, the back store, and the loft. This back shop area is where we assemble customers' orders and prepare goods before they go to the front shop. It's really a middle shop, as there's a big storage area at the back."

I noticed the boss's office was in a corner of the middle area with the two-bar electric heater near his door. Two big jute sacks hung on hooks on an area of the wall. Against a section of the wall was a fitment consisting of small drawers, all labelled with the names of spices.

The storage space at the rear was almost the same size of the front shop. This was the real back shop, where products were kept. I could see stacks of boxes all around. Freddie had told me to keep the message bike here.

"If you're ever asked to wash anything, this gas geyser gives immediate hot water to wash trays and plates for the provisions window, and this gas ring beside the sink is where you'll boil water for tea. When you sweep the floor here, always tidy around the sink and wash dirty cups," Cathie explained.

"Will somebody tell me when to sweep floors?"

"No, it's up to you to keep everything tidy. Now, let's go to the loft."

The steep wooden stairs were set against the side of the bare stone wall of the back store. I had to put my right hand on the wall as I climbed, as there was no hand rail. No strict health and safety regulations in those days!

"This is where we keep 'empties', such as biscuit tins, bottles and wooden tomato boxes."

A cobwebbed skylight window dominated, and I could see the roof joists with slate nails hammered through the sarking. It had a warm stale smell, but I imagined it would be cold in winter.

"We have a never-ending job catching mice here," Cathie said.

No wonder, I thought. Ideal conditions for mice to breed in a cosy place and enjoy lots of biscuit crumbs.

"While we're here, I'll show you how to deal with the mousetraps."

My jaw dropped. Mice? Traps? Oh, no! Then I noticed Cathie was carrying a paper bag and a small tray containing small cheese pieces. She pointed to three traps in different corners of the loft, and there was a mouse in each. Under supervision of Cathie's gaze, I nervously emptied the traps, dropped the mice into the bag as Cathie held it open, and reset the traps with fresh (well stale) cheese. Wow! That was a test I didn't expect.

"Well done. Now let's get outside." She unlocked the heavy back door, and we stepped out into sunlight. "This is the toilet. We share it with Cunningham the chemist next door who clean it, and they're quite fussy. Over here is where you have to flatten cardboard boxes and stack them up for the scaffies to take away."

"Where do I put the stuff in jute sacks, Cathie?"

"Yes, good question. Empty them into the biggest cardboard box you can find, and stamp it down as much as you can. I'll just put the mice in there now," she said without ceremony.

Partway along the corridor on the way back to the front shop, Cathie opened a door which led into a dingy space under the stair of the tenement above the shop.

"This is where you'll keep empty cardboard boxes for orders."

It had a damp, dank smell, and when I asked Cathie about it she replied: "It's been used only for storing empty boxes, but I was told it used to be a salt cellar."

I thought the tour was completed, but it wasn't.

"Now look, there's some sweeping to be done," said Cathie, pointing to scraps of paper on the floor. "I'll show you how to sweep a floor. Always push away from you like this. Now here's something else – how to brush rubbish on to a shovel in your other hand. Let me see you do it."

Shakily, I swept the paper waste with my right arm onto the shovel, but my uncoordinated left arm let the shovel slope allowing the sweepings to fall. After two more attempts I managed.

Cathie then pointed to the potato bin and said, "Keep watching the stock level. Bring supplies from the back shop when you see we're running low. Now you need to know what kind of paper bags we use here. You may be asked to bring them forward to the back shop." She pointed to various bags, and gave me a description of each. "We have one pound and half-pound biscuit bags, sweetie bags, strong large brown bags that we use for potatoes, and one pound cereal bags as well as one pound and two pound sugar bags. Then we have parchment paper for cooked meats and bacon."

My head was spinning. *I'll never remember all that*, I thought.

"Just one last thing today: the sun shades. They're put up first thing every morning using this long pole with a hook. But your job will be to take them down. The first thing you need to know is that the shades and the side shade go up every day, no matter what the weather. On week days you'll need to take the side shade down first at 6 o'clock. It's changed from the sunny morning side to this west side at lunch time. You see, it's hooked on at the wall and clipped into the big shade, so you need to use this folding chair to stand on. You'll do all the work with shades on Saturdays." Cathie demonstrated, and then showed me how to deal with the big shades. She gave a few up and down demonstrations while standing on the roadway. Then it was my turn.

"Remember, on Saturdays you'll deal with everything. Just keep in mind, sunny side first in the mornings for the side shade.

The boss was right. It was more than just doing deliveries. Would I remember everything?

On that first Thursday I had five orders, one of which was to Mrs Kilbride at Westhaven. "This customer has been away on holiday for the last two weeks, so you haven't seen her yet, but her order is bigger than usual," Cathie explained.

"That's alright," I said. "I'll find my way around Westhaven."

To get there, I had to cross the railway line at Station Road, but – as luck would have it – the crossing gates were closed, and I had to stop in the middle of the road. I saw the owner of The Bookstall, Mrs Miller, inside the shop and gave her a wave. She waved back, smiled, and jokingly mimed movements as if she was steering with handlebars. Unfortunately, the 4.45 train from Dundee was expected followed by the 4.55 from Aberdeen, and I knew the signalman would keep the gates closed for both. I had been very proud of my bookstall task, and I had time to think back affectionately to the day that job started about three years previously.

"It's a cauld nicht to be standing around here," said a tall thin man in the cluster of customers at the bookstall. "Gordon surely hasn't turned up the nicht," muttered the lady behind the counter.

Dad had asked me to run along to get the evening sports results newspaper. I was standing amongst a group of men who were, like me, waiting for the *Sporting Post*s to arrive. I didn't know Gordon, but – in the past – I'd seen him appear with newspapers.

"Could somebody run up the road to Christie's and see what's happened?" said the stall-holder.

"Here's a richt pair o' young legs here to run up the road," proclaimed a small, fat man pointing in my direction.

"Aye, son – would you like tae go to Christie's and see what ye can see? Be as quick as ye can."

**The Saturday *Sporting Post*
Run**

I knew Christie's was a newsagent but, as I set off, I'd no idea what to expect. When I arrived at the shop there was no one outside, but lying on the pavement was a rolled-up bundle of papers with the words 'Carnoustie Bookstall' written in thick black ink. I remember thinking that this must be what they're waiting for; it looks like the sort of thing Gordon used to deliver. I picked up the heavy roll and ran as fast as I could to the bookstall. When I was within yards of the queue, the men started to clap their hands and someone shouted out: "Well done son!"

"Where were they?" asked the owner.

"Lying on the pavement outside Christie's," I replied. The shop lady ran a knife up the outside wrapping paper and a coil of *Sporting Post*s unfolded. The men in the queue paid for their papers and walked away. Then it was my turn.

"*Sporting Post*, please," I requested as I handed over three pennies.

"Thanks, son. And here's something tae yersel." She handed me a threepenny piece. "You have a job if you want it, son. Be at Christie's at quarter to seven next Saturday to get the papers when they come off the van."

"Aye, I'll do that," not believing my luck that I'd earn another threepence. I rushed home to tell my dad the news.

"Oh, that's Mrs Miller behind the counter. Well, if you've said you'll do it then you'd better not let her down."

The following Saturday at half-past six I thought I should let Mrs Miller see I had turned up. "I'm here," I said when I approached the stall.

"Well done, son." As I stood at Christie's for a while, several men arrived and stood beside the door. Then a small red van screeched to a halt as the driver sounded the horn, quickly emerged, and threw out three bundles of papers of differing dimensions all tied together with thick hairy twine. They had hardly stopped rolling when Mr Christie cut the string with a knife and grabbed the thickest bundle, then ran back inside his shop. He was in a hurry to serve his customers. Then I saw someone pick up another bundle and I realised that must have been the delivery for Wood's, a newsagent that was a hundred yards along the street. I saw the Bookstall name and ran as fast as I could to the railway crossing. From the top of Station Road I could see the gathering of men who again applauded me as I approached. I got my threepence and paid for dad's paper, and while on my way along to West-haven I felt part of the fast chain of events to get the sports results from the printer to the customer.

My first paid job. I was nine years old, and had inad-vertently learned something about transport, distribution, customers and wages.

"I have to be there every Saturday at half-past six," I told mum.

"You'd better not let Mrs Miller down, now," she re-plied sternly.

Next thing I knew, a driver behind me was sounding his car horn and I was jolted out of my vivid memories. I re-started my journey and did my delivery to Westhaven with no problem. So far, I'd made no mistakes.

Then, on Friday as I was picking up a box, Cathie said: "Be careful with this delivery. Mrs McDonald's a very nice lady, but also very fussy."

On reaching the address I remembered Freddie's advice and parked on a level surface. It was a windy day, and suddenly there was a big gust which – catching the name plate broadsides – blew the bike over. The box flew out of the basket. Groceries were all over the muddy road, and a can of Granny's tomato soup did a slow-motion roll across the street into the gutter. I cleaned everything and repacked. The eggs – in a papier maché tray tied with string – seemed undamaged, but I wasn't sure. My stomach was turning. Had Mrs McDonald seen me from her window? I knocked on the door, and the stern face of my customer appeared.

As I handed over the box, I confessed and in my panic said: "I'm sorry, Mrs McKenzie. The wind blew my bike over."

She frowned. "I'm not Mrs McKenzie. I hope I've got the right order. Dear, oh dear; how did you manage that?"

"I'm sorry, Mrs McDonald. I made a mistake with the bike."

When she came back with the empty box, she said. "I've no change today, son."

Freddie had got a tip last week. This was bad news. Would she report me for being careless? Would she stop her orders? Sleep didn't come easily that night.

On Saturday evening the boss rushed past me while handing me my pay. He was chanting as he went, "Go, go, greasy grocer go." I stared at him, and then at my hand with thirteen shillings and sixpence in it. It seemed easy money for just pedalling around on a message bike. I'd earned four and three pence in tips, too! I started my savings in a decorated

Tate and Lyle syrup can. I didn't say anything, but I was aware of how scarce money was in the household. Despite mum and dad never saying anything, I could sense the problem. One day, I overheard mum saying to Isobel that she didn't have money to buy material to make a dress to wear for one of her new dances at her class, and on another I witnessed mum in tears telling Peem she couldn't replace the ruler he'd lost until the end of the week. Peem looked on in amazement as I handed over ten shillings to mum. Cold, wet days would come. Part of my first money was put aside with a plan to buy wellies, a yellow waterproof cycling cape and breeks.

I worried all the next week about Mrs McDonald, but on Friday as I was returning through the front shop she spotted me.

"Here's your shilling, son."

"Thanks, Mrs McDonald."

She was being served, and I noticed the stack of groceries on the counter. She was still shopping with us! Phew!

One day the following week I met Johnny Ross, the lad now doing the Co-op butchery job. He was slouching along the pavement, kicking an imaginary ball and looking miserable.

"How's it going, Johnny?"

"Terrible. It's just so boring!"

"Gee whiz!"

Well done, Jim! I couldn't help thinking how I narrowly escaped the Co-op job, and how Freddie asked Jim if he knew anybody to do his job. In all the things that were going wrong for me, something brilliant had happened when I least expected it. If it had been a rainy day I wouldn't have been drinking my milk on the school steps. Being in the right place at the right time – twice! – had kicked off my message boy career.

CHAPTER 3

More Than Deliveries, or "We'll Make a Wee Greasy Grocer Out of You Yet"

July/August 1953

THE first thing I did when I arrived at the shop one evening was knock on the boss's office door.

"Just to remind you, Mr Stewart – I'll be at my camp next week, and I've asked my brother James to stand in for me."

"Does he know the town well?" asked the boss sternly, looking me in the eye.

"Oh, yes – he's done a paper round too, so he won't make any mistakes."

"I hope not!"

I'd committed myself to attending the camp prior to being offered the message boy job, and though I didn't want to miss a week in the shop I had a feeling it would be my last Scout camp.

Annual summer Scout camps formed part of my year's activities. Peem and I were in different troops, so we didn't camp together. 'Tattie Thomson's' lorry was the regular form of transport to camps. It was scary, for we sat on an open-top lorry with no sides and travelled up to sixty miles away to our base. Tents, ground sheets, pots and pans along with our kit-bags were loaded first, and we sat on top with the wind (and occasionally rain) battering us. Camps were a hive of activity of cooking, cleaning, chopping wood and making fires. We became quite experienced Scouts, always aiming to achieve one more exciting Scout badge for semaphore signalling, mapping, woodsman or whatever.

Unforgettable moments were the early morning walks through the cold dewy grass on our way to the camp kitchen. More memorable ones were of cooking food over an open fire, and occasionally turning a rabbit on a spit.

We climbed mountains and, in the evenings – while wrapped in a blanket with a mug of hot cocoa in hand – sang songs seated around the big fire. The flag was lowered, and we sang 'Taps'. I can't imagine my life without having been a Scout. It had all started when Peem and I had become Cubs the evening mum took us to a party at our friends, the Reid's. Our pal Harry, already a Cub, invited us to go with him.

My troop camped in successive years at Glen Farg, Glen Clova and Pitlochry, and strangely enough as years passed we became more interested in where the nearest Girl Guide camps were located. I don't know why!

Mum's illness didn't become clear to me until parents' visiting day at my Scout camp in August. All the mums walking across a field towards our campsite were in summer clothes but my mum, noticeably, was wearing a long, wide coat. She carried a heavy looking bag which I guessed and hoped contained her home baking treats and some sweets for me, but she was lagging behind. I could see she needed assistance. Standing beside Skipper, my Scout master, I realised that I must help. After all, 'a Scout must help others at all times' was a law. There was no escape. I had to help her, but a combination of embarrassment and ignorance rooted me to the spot.

"Your mum's looking tired, Robert," said Skipper, suggesting I should help her.

"She's suffering from preggars," I explained, repeating what Jim had told me.

"You mustn't say that, Robert! That's not nice. You mean, she's expecting a baby."

"What?!"

"Yes, of course. Now off you go and help her."

The moment I approached mum and took the bag from her hand was the first time I acknowledged the unthinkable fact. Yes, mum must be expecting a baby. None of my pals or my Scout master made any comment about it, but after that day I lived with the inescapable situation.

I didn't know whether to laugh or cry. Jim was right after all, but mum wasn't going to die and preggars wasn't an illness.

Returning from camp late on Friday afternoon I couldn't wait to speak with Peem about his message boy work, but when I walked into the house – complete with my kit bag and a bundle of clothes for washing – I was in for a shock.

"I'm home, mum!" I called as I entered the living room.

"Oh, you must be Robert. I'm Mrs Taylor. Your mum asked me to make your tea tonight," said the tall, friendly stranger who was busy setting the table.

"Where's mum?" was my first shocked reaction as I laid my things on the floor.

"She's at the doctors, and may be a while in the queue," said the person in a strange, unfamiliar voice.

Then I recalled that mum had said holiday visitors would be coming soon, and – thanks to my understanding Scout master – I quickly accepted the fact mum would probably need to see a doctor.

"Is mum not well?" I asked the pleasant stranger.

"Your mum's fine. Nothing to worry about."

Just then I was in for another jolt. An unknown man and two boys – one lean, who I thought looked about my age, and another, smaller and more plump – came into the house. I guessed they must be the husband and children who had come to stay. It was all quite overwhelming, but they were friendly and I knew this was one of mum's ways of making some extra money, so I had to happily accept the intrusion.

"We got here a bit early from Falkirk," said Mrs Taylor as she continued to stir something in a pot. "This is Charles," indicating the older boy, "and this is Iain."

I was glad to get to my room and check on my tadpoles, which Peem had been charged to look after, when I heard laughter from the living room and he suddenly appeared.

"How did you get on?" I asked.

"Great! I was paid the same as you and I made over two pounds tips. But your boss is a strange man. He even told me I had to speak properly to customers – no 'kens' and 'cannies'."

"You just have to get used to him," I replied.

The next day mum ask me to help her.

"Dad's on relief duty at the signal box at Carnoustie West, and he's on a normal day shift from 9 o'clock until five so he can't be home for lunch. Can you cycle along and deliver his lunch?"

"That's alright, mum. When do you want me to go?"

"Just as soon as you can," she said, wrapping sandwiches in a bag.

Mum then filled a bowl with hot soup and placed parchment paper over it, tightly tying string around the rim.

"Now don't go fast over the bumpy road along by the golf course and spill the soup," she added as she placed everything in a basket to fit on the front of my bike.

I still remember how slow I had to travel to make sure dad's lunch reached him as mum planned. He seemed happy with it, and asked me if I wanted to watch him changing the signals. He had his soup and sandwiches and was constantly interrupted by bells ringing and him sending coded messages on a gadget – a bit like I'd seen Morse code being used in war films. I could see that it was not easy to pull the signal levers, which were about four feet long with a shiny steel handle at the top and a small, lever-like clutch. This had to be pulled to release a catch before the lever could be pulled about three feet towards him to raise a stop signal and show a red light. A signal in the down position showed a green light.

Years later, dad told me that a signal in the down position was dangerous as it could be down simply because a wire was broken, and so the procedure was reversed to pull a signal into an up position with a green light

"Can I try to pull a lever, dad?" I said, after I saw him put one foot up on a rail to give greater leverage.

"You'll need to wait until we have to."

It was my first time in a signal box, and I asked dad questions I'd always had in mind. How do you know when a train is coming? Do you need to speak on the phone to other signalmen? How do you know which levers to pull? His answers sounded quite simple, but I realised how vitally accurate the procedures had to be. When eventually he asked me to pull a lever, I found it impossible and he had to take hold of the long handle and pull with me. I cycled home with great admiration of the importance of the job he did, and started to dread the day there was a train crash when he was on duty.

* * *

I couldn't wait to get back into the shop after my holiday, and when I did I had the immediate impression that it was busier than ever. On the Thursday evening, Cathie had news for me.

"Now, Robert, here's an order for another new customer: Mrs Crerar," she said, pointing to a large filled box. "She wants her delivery after five o'clock."

Customers' requests had to be acknowledged, and although there was a recognised sequence of deliveries I was free to plan new routes. Each Sunday, after our special lunch, mum and dad took us on family walks around the town and country areas, which was an unwitting way of learning roads and local geography. All that history served me well.

My new cape, wellies and breeks proved valuable on many occasions, but I had no headgear. I felt the need to wear a bonnet, but I wasn't sure what kind. One evening I asked mum if she would buy me a hat.

"My goodness. Why don't you spend some of your savings?"

"Can I not have one of dad's caps?"

"No. They're not suitable."

"If you don't want to spend your own money, try this on," mum said after tea, casually handing me a beret.

"It's got a toorie on it. It's a lassie's hat! I canna wear that, mum!"

Mum, probably anticipating my response, swiftly took the beret and snipped off the toorie.

"There. Is that any better?"

Viewing it in the mirror, I jumped with joy.

"That's great! None of the other message laddies ha'e anything like that!"

Deep down, I thought I knew why. Nevertheless, Mum's maroon beret became my everyday practical headgear.

* * *

I'd encountered a few thunder storms, but it was always comfortable – especially on colder days, when the sea haar blocked out the sun – to return to the back shop and warm myself beside the two-bar electric heater.

"This is your cup. Just help yourself from the pot," said Dot one cold wet day when I'd forgotten my pullover. "You can pull out this drawer and use it as a seat while you have your cuppa." She tugged at the drawer handle on the bench where the orders were assembled.

"Thanks, Dot," I said as I sat on the sharp edge of the drawer while she propped herself on top of a wooden crate of New Zealand Cheese.

The practice seemed to be that the teapot was placed on top of the electric fire, even when it wasn't switched on.

Wow! I suddenly felt part of the team.

"You're allowed to buy your own biscuits, you know. Ayton Sandwiches are a penny, and Wagon Wheels threepence."

Both became my favourites.

Although my exits and returns were made through the front shop, I made sure I didn't loiter around there. All the action was in the front shop, where business was done. That was the public place where discussions, requests and dialogue between staff and customers went on. I'd come to realise that the shop was prepared in advance with all stock in place and window displays set up, and when blinds went up it signalled that the shop and staff were ready for business. At the end of the day, when blinds went down the shop and staff were once again in a private place. It was the distinction between private and public which gave me the idea that it seemed like a stage, with the customers being the audience. I saw myself as part of the back shop, so I kept out of sight.

On entering the shop, I was always aware of fresh fruit and confectionery aromas from the right hand side and smoked bacon and dairy smells of butter and cheese on the left. The strongest scent was the nose-tingling minty one of fresh tomatoes, which were displayed in baskets on a slim table positioned at the front door. In good weather both parts of the front door were open, and a display of vegetables stretched several yards from the doorstep all the way to the counter.

"Now, Robert, if you're here at closing time then move the door displays into the middle of the floor space. Go, go, greasy grocer go," said the boss one evening as he dashed past me.

Mr Stewart's strange behaviour became commonplace to me. Somehow his actions reflected the pace of shop life, while at other times I felt he set the pace. It was difficult to work it out; perhaps he was reflecting the frantic pulse of the business. When all the staff were serving at the counter, I heard the banter and the jingling of the cash register. Once it quietened, staff would return to the back shop and continue with their jobs. Soon I started helping, and was praised when they returned to find I'd finished a job for them.

When all staff were fully engaged with customers, I was aware of them rushing back and forth between the front and back shop. As I stood there watching, it seemed wrong that I was being paid to do nothing, so I made myself busy by finding jobs to do.

Always have something to do was, I felt, the right attitude. Don't hang about.

"Thanks for taking those boxes to the back shop, Robert," Isobel said one busy evening.

"That's alright. I was waiting to get an order checked, so I filled in the time."

"Now, Robert, my wee greasy grocer; go to the loft and sort out all the biscuit tins into names," said the boss one evening.

"What does that mean?" I asked nervously.

"Well, you'll see names on tins. McFarlane Lang, Weston, Crawford, Carr's, McVitie & Price – oh yes, and Jacobs. Just put them all into separate lots, and then put all the Crawford's tins inside the back door. There's a delivery coming tomorrow, and we'll get money back for empties."

This was the first real job the boss had asked me to carry out. When he said he'd get money back, I realised it was important and that I couldn't afford to make any mistakes. It was an early example of me having to earn my worth, and I had to concentrate on what he was saying. As I did the job, I noticed big tins were cube shaped, about twelve inches square. Half-tins were only six inches deep. Biscuits, I had noticed earlier, were loose in tins and staff had to pick out them out and weigh whatever the customer asked. There was always a risk of breaking them while in the wicker basket on the bike.

"Well done. Now just keep an eye on all these tins in the loft and sort them by their names," the boss said when I had finished. It was another new job for me to do, and I wondered why Freddie hadn't been doing it. Maybe he didn't like the loft smells, or was scared by mice – or both! While I was sorting tins, I saw empty bottles were all mixed up, so I tidied them into groups: Lemonade, Parazone, and Ammonia.

"Who sorted the bottles?" said the boss as he went whizzing past a day or two later.

"It was me," I said warily.

"Oh, well done! We'll make a wee greasy grocer of you yet," he said as he disappeared.

Meanwhile, the Taylor family – all occupying one bedroom – seemed to enjoy themselves. Because both families ate together, I picked up all the things they were happily experiencing around the town. It was as if they had come from another planet. Falkirk didn't mean much to me, but their words and dialect were very different. Yet they seemed to have fallen in love with Westhaven.

"Charles wants to go fishing with you before he goes home, Robert," mum said as she and Mrs Taylor tidied dishes at the sink.

"That's good," I said. "The tide will be far out tomorrow evening."

After my usual Friday deliveries, I rushed home for tea and changed into my fishing clothes and old sandals with the cut-out toes that I used for wading across the rocks.

"Be careful, now. Charles won't know the rocks, and watch you don't get cut off by the tide," mum said in her usual nervous way.

I quickly dug up some bait while explaining the routine to Charles. Whilst all this was commonplace for me, I guessed it must have been like a trip to the moon for Charles, who seemed to come from a land of coal mines and canals.

"Gee, I can't wade out any further 'cos I can't see where to put my feet," Charles said.

"Don't worry; we'll wait for the tide a bit. This is Poddlie and that's Dargie, and over there is Limpy," I told a confused Charles as we sat down to await the tide receding.

"How did they get these names?" he asked while he followed my advice about how to bait his hook and where to fish. I told him how my fishing days on the rocks had started, and my mind went back to the day Jim started me off.

It was summer 1950, and the start of a period of expanding boundaries and growing responsibility. School holidays had begun, and I hadn't seen Jim since playing on the rocks with him the previous year. He was on his way home from fishing off the rocks, and he was carrying his rod and line.

"What's that you've got there, Jim?"

"It's a wee cod."

"Jings, I wish I could get oot on the rocks wi' you."

"Well, ask yer mum and tell her ye'll be wi' me."

"Can I get on the rocks to fish, mum? Jim said he would look after me."

"Did he? Well, ask him to come here and speak to me."

I ran to his house and asked him.

"I'll be roond later, Robbie."

"Will you watch the tides? Will you not go too far out and get cut off? Will you come in when I call you?" mum quizzed Jim.

"Aye, I'll look efter him, Mrs Murray," said Jim, having satisfactorily answered all mum's questions.

Peem overheard all this.

"Can me and Coffie come tae, mum?"

"Is that alright with you Jim?"

"If they dae whit I tell them, it'll be aricht."

The way was clear. The word went around and – as if from nowhere – Peem, Coffie and Ollie appeared. Jim handed us all bits of line and gut which the fishermen had given him, and he passed us hooks which he had spare.

"You'll need tae get bits o' bamboo cane for rods oot o' yer dad's gairden. Now ye need tae watch the tide times. Keep looking at the newspaper and ye'll see Dundee high and low tide times – we're an hour later here at the Ha'en. Come wi' me the morn aboot ten o'clock, and we'll dig some bait. Bring a spade and wee bucket. But we'll no get fishin' till the tide goes back. We'll start to walk oot on the rocks aboot twelve o'clock."

Jim turned up early and fixed us all up with our fishing rods, which we left at my place, and our procession made its way to the harbour. The tide had started to recede, and we followed it out.

"Now, do ye see these worm casts?"

Jim pointed with his spade to thin, sandy threads coiled on the sand.

"That's lug worm. Watch whit I dae." Jim dug a trench about a spade deep and about two feet long and, as it filled with sea water, he splashed it over the pile of sand and the worms became visible. We soaked up all his advice and collected as much bait as he advised.

"Now, we go back tae yer hoose, Robbie, collect the rods and get oot on the rocks. Oh aye, just wear yer sandshoes – nae socks. Ye need something tae walk on the sharp rocks."

"Our dad cuts the taes aff oor last year's sandals," I said on behalf of Peem and myself.

"But we havnae got our new sandals this year yet," added Peem.

"Sand shoes and nae socks'll be fine for noo," said Jim.

"I've only got wellies," Ollie mentioned.

"Nae good, Ollie. But it'll have tae dae the day."

The excitement was uncontainable. I was now allowed by mum, after all those years, to go far out on the rocks. We watched patiently as the water went back. Jim pointed out what we needed to know.

"There's Poddlie – that's the first high rock we get on to. From there we wade oot and get on tae Limpy, then on to Dargie." Jings! Jim even had names for the rocks.

We got onto Poddlie, named after a poddle (small cod) Jim had seen there. While we waited for the tide to go back, he showed us how – using a second bucket – he drained the pools on the rock so we could catch little fish. Then the wait to get on to Limpy, so called because it was covered in limpet shells. Jim waded out into deep water and climbed on.

"How do you know where to walk?" I called out.

"Aye, that's the trick. Ye have to practise where to put yer feet when there's nae water there."

We all caught up with him and fished there for a while, though with no luck. It became obvious why we needed sandshoes, as the rocks were covered by sharp shells – mainly limpets and some mussels.

Jim again walked through deep water and arrived on Dargie, which was the ultimate target. Once there he explained that dargies were young poddles – about six inches long, with a dark green back and a silvery white underbelly.

"We were finally all on Dargie, ready at long last to start fishing. That's how it started for me, Charles."

"Did you catch any fish?" Charles asked.

"Well, this is where the dangers of fishing off the rocks is real. You see, we were catching dozens of dargies and were so engrossed that we didn't see the tide turn. Jim screamed out a warning, and we picked up our buckets and ran. In the rush, Ollie tried to jump across a gap in the rocks and fell in. He disappeared completely under the water, and we rushed to the spot. He came up gasping for air but sank again. Jim pushed us aside and grabbed Ollie by the hair when he reappeared and laid him on a rock. Poor Ollie was retching and gurgling, and his face turned a bluish white. Jim punched his back and Ollie began to breathe. Then we noticed Ollie had lost his wellies.

Saving Ollie

"I remember Jim's words to this day, Charles. 'You see, lads? Wellies are no good. Lucky he lost them. He'd be drooned if he hadnae'."

"Was Ollie in trouble with his mum?"

"No, Jim made us promise to say Ollie had got stuck in mud and lost his wellies. So better not tell my mum that story."

I told Charles as much as I could remember; he started using the rock names, and his excitement grew as he started to pull out a dargie every few minutes.

"You've landed lucky tonight, Charlie. We might start calling this spot 'Charlie's Rock'."

Charlie told his mum and dad all about it, and said he wanted to move so that he could live in Carnoustie.

"No, we can't do that, son," his dad said. "We'll just have to keep coming back in the summer."

* * *

When not out delivering, other tasks filled my time such as polishing the brass scales and weighing up sugar. It was delivered loose in bags weighing two hundred-weights, and had to be packaged into one pound or two pound brown bags tied with string. A constant job was to move stock from the back store to the preparation area, ready to replenish front shop shelves. Each time I had an opportunity, I began to keep a close watch on stock levels. The trick was to see how fast something was selling and gauge when restocking was needed. I worked out what needed attention and when. In a strange way, I found it was simply about guessing priorities and making decisions.

Some suppliers delivered goods from vehicles parked at the front of the shop. On such occasions, stock was stored in the middle area taking up nearly all available floor space. It was easy to see the big rush to pack goods on shelves to make room to assemble and check customer orders. I could tell it was a difficult balance – what was most important: orders or restocking? I could see that both were essential, but failing to deliver an order on time was more serious. Sometimes a delivery was so big that staff had to climb over boxes or squeeze through spaces. It simply slowed everything down. The root of the problem was that there was insufficient road space at the rear of the shop to bring stock into the back store from big lorries. That, I thought, would have solved the problem.

Once staff had assembled an order, I was often given the job of calling off the goods listed on the invoice. As the goods were being checked off, they were packed by one of the staff who talked me through how to load the box. Heavy items such as potatoes and canned goods went on the bottom, smelly soap wrapped separately in newspaper, eggs and biscuits on top, and so on. Although orders were different, those basic rules applied.

Each day had its own character, with a mixture of different jobs and routes. Orders were either phoned in or purchased at the counter, and occasionally a late, unplanned order would mean a rush to deliver and return before six o'clock closing.

There were two very large orders which didn't go into cardboard boxes. Each order filled the wicker basket to the brim.

The ladies packed the goods into the basket and the boss helped me carry it and place it on the bike.

"Now, Robert, remember you'll get a hand to carry the basket at the other end. Do you feel safe with that?"

"Yes, I'm fine."

"Well now, take it easy and don't run out of control. Go, go, greasy grocer go!"

Mr Stewart hastily went back inside, leaving me to pedal off at a cautious speed and recalling Freddie's clever advice about keeping tyres hard.

Both 40 minute round trip uphill deliveries were on Saturdays and into the countryside, and were tiring – especially on cold, wet or windy days. But the reward was a half crown tip at each. One was to Muirdrum via Battie's Den. This was tough, as it was a fast run downhill followed by a dangerous sharp left bend over a bridge, then an exhausting walk uphill pushing the bike. The other delivery was to Travebank, an old staging post on the main Dundee to Arbroath Road.

It was those deliveries which gave me the idea of classifying all my runs into either level or uphill. While on those runs, I could picture Miss Main – my respected geography teacher – standing smartly dressed beside the blackboard, telling us precisely about the raised beach that runs parallel with the coast and divides the town into low and high level. When I had an uphill journey I used to mutter to myself: "Raised beach equals raised effort."

There was a new, unusual delivery I had to make to the bothy at Westhaven farm. It was for two young, single employees – farm hands – and they each had their own order. This delivery was to the extreme east end of the town – in fact, the last building on that boundary – and it made me think of the distance between my furthest west and east customers. My estimate was three miles and, with the two miles inland journey to Muirdrum, I calculated that my cycling area was about six square miles.

"Put both boxes inside the big wooden kist on the floor in front of the window, and make sure you close the lid," instructed Cathie.

"Why is that?"

"To stop the mice eating the groceries before the lads get home."

Not another mouse problem! I thought.

The door had no lock, nor was there gas or electric light. I lifted the heavy wooden top of the kist and – with my nose itching by the immediate strong smell of mouldy food and old straw placed the boxes inside the kist – glanced around the bare wooden floor and rough meagre furnishings in the stale, sweaty one-room building. That's when I spotted the only bed, with a striped cloth mattress spilling straw out of its punctured side. I was distracted by the pitiful state, and my imagination worked overtime as I theorised that this was where the mice lived. That may have been as big a problem as sharing a bed with your workmate. What was worse – the mice or the mate? Or was it both?

In preparation for deliveries on dark winter nights, I started to walk with my eyes closed towards the bothy, open the door and walk to the kist. I did keep my eyes open a tiny crack as I trained myself to steer clear of obstacles, people or mice – or all three! On my way back to the shop, however, I rationalised that it would be best to make noises to scare the mice before I felt one running over my feet while inside the bothy.

There seemed to be new customers every week. My pockets began to bulge with tips, and I hurried home to count my pennies as I dropped them into the syrup can.

CHAPTER 4

New Jobs, or "Blinds Up, Robert!"

October 1953

"ANOTHER new customer, Robert – Mrs Brown at South America," said Cathie.

"Jings! Where will I get the boat?" I said jokingly to Cathie, knowing full well it was the name of a group of cottages on the golf course.

"She says the bell doesn't work; you have to open the door and shout."

This was just another new route with a difference, as this time I had to beware of golfers playing on the second hole of the Burnside course. I had played there with Peem, and I knew that golfers had to take care not to hit vehicles or people as they crossed over to the cottages. But mistakes happen...

As weeks passed bringing early winter winds and rain, my waterproofs and mum's maroon beret served me well. With the shop located about halfway along the main street, cycling was exhausting – especially when wearing my bulging yellow cape – but it was wonderful to glide along effortlessly with the wind, not least when the wicker basket was fully loaded.

One evening, the tiny red thread of my rear lamp element finally died. I'd been following my dad's advice and surreptitiously putting the battery on the warm electric fire in the back shop in frequent attempts to prolong its life, but now it really was dead. Recalling Freddie's warning, I plucked up the courage one evening to ask the boss for money to buy a battery.

"Well, well my wee greasy grocer? You don't need a new battery already, do you?"

"Yes," I stammered, praying that my front lamp would keep going a few more weeks.

"Off you go to Clark's and bring me a receipt and the change," he said as he opened the till drawer and handed me a florin.

Within minutes, I was standing inside the cycle shop with the smell of oil, new rubber and the industrious Mr Clark's greasy stained jacket, hoping that the florin would cover the cost while reminding myself to get a receipt. On my way back to the shop I met Norrie, a classmate who worked for Harry McKay's grocery business further along the High Street. Meeting other message lads was a joy. We exchanged tales of biggest orders up the steepest hills, and the highest speeds down. I think I won the former, but Norrie – with his clever, daredevil cycling skills – won the latter. Who was earning the best tips? That seemed to be an equal result, but I was never sure who was telling the biggest fibs. Likewise, the most orders delivered in one evening also seemed a pretty close thing, but quietly I thought I won that. What I noticed was that my wicker basket was the biggest. Everyone else had what was called a half-size (or 'butcher's') basket. I could have teased them and called them 'butcher's boys', but I kept quiet about it because it would probably be deemed a disadvantage, and my pals would probably say: "It's nae use, 'cos it hids ye back on windy days."

When we chatted about our duties I discovered we all carried out an odd request reflecting friendly cooperation between shops, which I'm sure wouldn't happen today. As an example, when a customer ordered a can of tomato soup, but we were sold out, I would be sent off to another grocery shop in the town with a can of kidney soup to do a swap. This would start gentle banter between the competing shop staff and myself about price comparisons, and teasing about running out of stock. Of course, occasionally a competing message lad would come to us.

"Your boss lost the plot about re-ordering again?" Jock Brown, one of my classmates, would tease.

"Our amazing sales growth must be greater than yours!" I always replied.

I developed a loyalty to my shop, and found myself defending my boss.

Jock was the message boy for a small shop, which was probably the best high-class grocer and wine merchant in the town. It was a store with a select clientele, and Jock – with his bright, theatrical mind – had, for fun, developed a 'posh' personality and always seemed to want to top any story I had. In fact, he tried to top stories told by all the message lads. We enjoyed exchanging banter. His most impressive claim was that his boss was considering fitting a dynamo on his bike. I knew instinctively Jock was making this up to tease us. In those days, front and rear lights lit by a dynamo was a real plus, but we all laughed and said it would never happen. In discussion, it was interesting to discover that other lads had battery problems too. It was with Jock that I seemed to have greatest contact, and I always found him to be sharp, clever and engaging with his cheeky tongue-in-cheek remarks. According to him, his shop's range of cheeses was much greater than mine, and they didn't sell bacon – only specially cured hams. His teas and coffees were more upmarket, and of course his shop stocked wines from around the world whereas Willie Lows didn't stock wines and spirits at all. Volume of sales was where I won my friendly arguments, and I began to develop a range of questions to throw at him when we met on our rounds. With no proof, I always suspected I could win with products such as eggs, cooked meats, bacon, fruit and vegetables. One day I used butter, because I knew exactly how many boxes I had opened.

"How much butter did you sell last week, Jock?" I prompted.

"Oh, just the usual – maybe three boxes of twenty eight pounds," he said defensively.

"Gee whiz! Is that all?" I teased cheekily. "We sold a hundredweight of New Zealand, fifty-six pounds of Danish, and nearly the same of Dutch." Jock would always reply boastfully and play the quality card.

"Ah, yes – but remember, Robbie, we sell only the best. And it's wrapped; not like that cheap stuff on the slab!"

Sometimes other staff asked me to help them lift heavy items, and I was called upon to assist. The most difficult boxes were Iraqi pitted and preserved whole dates, which were packed in wooden boxes with a gross weight of seventy pounds. Measuring about thirty inches long by roughly fifteen inches square, they were awkward to handle. Hammer and pliers were needed to undo the many nails and tough wire. The dates were in five layers of fourteen pounds each, very sticky, and separated by waxed paper. The sickly sweet smell of the syrup wafted towards me when I opened the box, and I tried to imagine Iraq and the people who had packed the fruits. To prevent sticky hands for staff, while serving a customer the dates were weighed in one pound bags and put in a drawer behind the counter.

One day I used Iraqi dates as a joust with Jock.

"Of course, Robbie, we sell packets – not that unhygienic stuff that's stamped into boxes by barefooted desert people," was his instant response.

While I was in bed that night, I couldn't help wondering how the date box was filled in Iraq. Now, thousands of miles away, it was opened by me – and thankfully I couldn't see any footprints. Other dried fruits such as sultanas, currants and raisins were similarly dealt with. Their countries of origin fascinated me: Greece, Australia, America and Syria. Cereals such as haricot and kidney beans, split peas, green peas and lentils, scooped out of fifty-six pound sacks, were also packed into one pound bags. All this was done by staff in time gaps when not serving customers.

As I became more involved in messy jobs, my mum complained that my school clothes were becoming mucky. Freshly laundered and starched white coats were delivered weekly to the shop, but there wasn't one for the message laddie. I hit on the idea of using the spare white apron I'd set aside at home for use during technical subjects at school. When I wore it, I really felt I was more than half a grocer. Well, an ounce of a grocer. I'd not seen Jock Brown wear a white apron or coat yet, so even on short journeys along the High Street I started wearing my apron hoping to meet him.

It was my own way of starting to compete. Or, more accurately, show off!

One evening the boss asked if I would work full-time during the forthcoming two week October school holiday.

"How would you like to be a full-time greasy grocer?" he said as he sped past. "You'll be paid two pounds ten shillings each week."

"Brilliant!" was my instant reply.

Previously I had done tattie picking during the October holiday, but this was a better option so I agreed because I would see more of what went on in the shop.

"You need to know the hours," added the boss. "We're open at 8.30 am to 12.45 pm, and then 2.15 pm 'til 6 pm every day. On half days, we open 8.30 am 'til 12 midday."

* * *

"Now it's time for you to learn the Monday morning window wash," said Cathie when I arrived at 8.30 on my first day of the tattie holidays.

"Fill up the galvanised bucket with warm water and put in some detergent, and take a second bucket of cold water with you. Use this long-handled brush and soap-wash the whole window, then wash the sides of the frames," she instructed as she washed the fruit window.

"Now go over the window with clean water and wash off the soap."

This she did, then asked me to do the provisions window.

"Now do the windows at the doorway," she requested as we moved to the back store. "It's really best to finish off by throwing some cold water over the windows, as it gets rid of any streaks. I haven't got the strength, but you would manage that?"

"Alright, I'll try."

Returning to the back store, I filled the buckets then successfully dealt with the fruit window. Sadly, my luck ran out when I threw water over the provisions window. Failing to check the situation, a customer – Mrs Roy – was drenched by my over-enthusiastic effort just as she emerged from the shop.

"Oh, my new tammy!" she called out.

I knew her, and all I could say was: "Sorry, Mrs Roy!" She was a friend of my mum, and I remember thinking I'd be lucky if my misdemeanour went unnoticed as I was forever aware of an obvious small town syndrome.

"I thought I told you to look after my customers," the boss said with a glint in his eye as he hurried past me on his way to the back store later.

"I'm sorry, but I did apologise to Mrs Roy. It's my mum I'm scared of," I said, feeling both guilty and silly.

My next job which Cathie explained was to use a hard brush to sweep the excess water on the roadway, then scrub the rubber 'Be-Ro' flour mats situated about the front shop floor and finish off by mopping.

"That's the big clean done now," said Cathie. "But remember, dry off the floor with a cloth wrapped around a brush head. We don't want any more accidents." Point taken.

My full-time week was brilliant, as I learned even more aspects of the business – especially what went on all through the day. Now every day, rain or shine, I put the shades up and down and switched over the side shade at lunchtime. Somehow a window blinds routine started when the boss would say "blinds up, Robert", and of course the reverse in the evenings if I was around at that moment. To me the blinds signalled the start and stop of being open for business. In my mind, they were like curtains for a stage performance.

Another new job was to go to the bank with the previous day's takings and collect bags of change. I was still at the bottom of the pecking order, but felt part of the team and was earning my cups of tea.

Now I was around on Tuesdays to see the large warehouse delivery from head office arrive, and could make an impact to help the staff. A flat-bed lorry complete with a tarpaulin cover delivered goods to the front door, which meant every item had to be carried in through the shop. As Tuesday was the half-day, the impact of a large delivery was keenly felt as everyone had to climb over boxes and squeeze through narrow spaces until staff had time away from the counter to pack stock on shelves.

"Give Eddie a help to hand-ball the easy things," said the boss. Eddie was the driver, and it was the first time I'd heard the term which simply meant carry one box at a time by hand as opposed to using a barrow. Another new experience awaited.

"Now Robert, here's a special order to deliver. You'll need to do it in three runs," said the boss one day while I was flattening cardboard boxes. "Do you know where the jam factory is?"

"Yes; the Jammy's in Thistle Street." Which I knew, by bike, was only ten minutes away. "How many boxes, Mr Stewart?"

"No, not in boxes. This is forty dozen eggs and fifty-six pounds of sugar. The sugar's made up in seven pound brown bags, and you'll have to be careful with the eggs."

This large order worried me, especially with so many eggs all in moulded papier mache trays with thirty eggs on each and stacked one on top of each other in my basket. They looked precarious to me and, realising it was a very windy day and with the Mrs McDonald bad experience behind me, I took extra care.

"You'll be alright; just take your time. I'll help you to pack your basket and, when you arrive, ring the bell and ask for help," the boss said supportively.

"What do they need all this for?" I enquired, as I couldn't see the relevance of eggs and sugar.

"They're making lemon curd this week. The berry jam season's past."

I didn't say anything and just accepted that eggs and sugar must be part of the ingredients.

"But where's the lemons?" I asked as an afterthought.

"They must be planning to use essence."

Another piece of learning for me and luckily, despite the wind, all three trips went well. My factory bulk delivery would be an interesting story to boast about to Jock. So far this had been my scariest mission, but it was regarded as a business delivery so there was no tip.

There were morning routines when I helped to prepare stock for window and doorway displays. Last duties in the evenings were to wash up counters and provisions plates and dishes.

* * *

"Don't be late tonight, Robert. Remember it's Saturday, and you and James will have to have your bath," said mum at lunchtime. "Dad's not here, so you'll both need to do all the work for me."

"We'll manage, mum. We've done it all before."

This was another way in which I had come to accept mum's condition. What she meant was that Peem and I had to follow strict rules about the use of the communal wash-house. When we moved to Westhaven in 1947, I became aware of striking contrasts between living there and in Annfield Cottage: one was that living in an upstairs flat required us to move about quietly. Mum repeatedly reminded us of her two golden rules – don't jump hard onto the floor, and don't be noisy on the stairs.

I soon learned that an important part of tenement life was the organisation and use of the wash-house. This was a separate, substantial standalone red brick building at the rear of the block of flats beside the spacious drying green complete with clothes poles at each corner. Mum was, with the agreement of neighbours, allowed to use the wash-house and drying green on Tuesdays, which was the day the previous occupants of our flat had been allocated. She had to use her own clothes line and pegs, but was permitted to use the stretchers which were kept inside the wash-house. Mum used them to push up and stretch the clothes line, which prevented clothes from touching the ground. The wash-house was fitted out with a large metal tub cemented into a stone block in the corner of the wash-house. The tub was shaped like an upturned dome, around three feet in diameter and nearly two feet deep, in which gallons of water were heated by means of a fire in a space at the bottom of the tub. I used to think it looked like a witch's cauldron. There was also a long deep bath in the opposite corner. Mum boiled some clothes in the tub, but she also – by using a bucket – filled another smaller sink with hot water where she rubbed clothing on a scrubbing board in soapy water. She then had to rinse clothes in cold water in an adjacent sink. Prior to hanging sheets and clothes on the line, she had to put garments through a mangle to squeeze out as much water as possible. The mangle, which was her own property, consisted of two rollers through which she fed the sheets and clothing. By turning a handle, she could press out the water. The wash-house always had a distinct fresh, warm, soapy, steamy smell on wash days and bath nights – a pleasant place to be, especially in winter. None of the other tenants made use of the bath and, on Saturday evenings, mum put a blanket across the window and Peem and I had a bath together. Afterwards the rest of the family had a turn.

"Wrap this blanket round you and run upstairs. Your pyjamas are warming by the fire," mum would say.

As cycling was the main form of transport, nearly everyone in the block had a bike. All bicycles used by the four families in the block were kept in the wash-house. It was essential they were put into the wash-house each evening in the precise order they were to come out in the morning. Mr and Mrs McLagan, the hard-working couple who lived below us, had to have their bikes put in last at night so that they were immediately accessible at seven o'clock in the morning, as they had to cycle to work at Carnoustie Laundry at the other end of the town. If my dad happened to be on late shift his bike would go in last, but he or mum would have to go downstairs the next morning and move it out before the McLagans needed their bikes out. Peem and I also had to have our bikes available for a 7 am start. Dad always had to make sure he could get his bike out first if he was cycling somewhere to start his early shift at six o'clock. Bikes were a constant part of everyday conversation.

Following these washhouse and bike rules, and mum's procedure for a bath night, Peem and I prepared for our weekly plunge. We removed all the bikes, and then – using a bucket – filled the wash tub with cold water and set a fire in the space underneath. When the water was heated and after we'd removed dust and spiders, we used buckets to fill the bath then add cold water until we had a comfortable temperature. With the heat from the fire and the steam which developed, the washhouse was a luxurious place to be. Only one thing went wrong the night Peem and I organised our own bath. I jumped in first.

"Peem!" I screamed. "You forgot to put the blanket across the window!"

"Sorry!" he said with a smile as he draped the blanket, which left me thinking he'd played a trick on me.

* * *

I was about to pick up the box of groceries for Mrs Clark, a regular customer who lived close to the beach on the sea side of the railway line at Bleachfield, when Cathie gave me a stern piece of advice.

"Now, did you hear about the railwayman who was killed on the line last week?"

"Yes, my dad told me."

"Well, he was knocked down by a train; he didn't hear it coming because of the noise of the wind he faced. So be very careful when you cross the railway, as it's a stormy night."

Cathie was referring to the fact that I had to push my bike with a loaded basket across the line at Bleachfield, which was a remote area about a mile outside the town. I had developed my own routine – I parked my bike on its stand, opened both large swing gates, and went back for my bike. I pushed it across the line then went back to close both gates, and then followed the same procedure on my return. My biggest worry was that the small wheel of the bike would get caught on the track. There was never anyone around and it was quite scary, but I never told mum I had that weekly delivery.

The number of orders continued to grow. The branch was winning new customers and creating a surge in sales. The boss seemed pleased with the growth, and I was secretly pleased to play my own little part in it. I began to feel that perhaps I was moving in the direction of being a greasy grocer after all.

CHAPTER 5

Increasing Skills, or "Skin That Cheese Now, Robert!"

October 1953

THE footsteps behind me seemed to speed up and become louder. I was on my way home alone from Scouts and walking along the lengthy and narrow Tayside Street at half-past eight. I was terrified, and dared not look behind me because I knew all I would see would be blinking street gaslights, shadows of bushes, and trees billowing across the road. I had often looked back, but each time I did the person following me had disappeared into a black shadow somewhere. This was not the only time I had these spooky feelings; it had been going on for weeks – since the dark nights started.

"Why do I have these feelings I'm being followed?" I finally asked dad one evening, after enduring the agony on a particularly windy moonless night.

"It's probably the echo of your own footsteps. The space between the high wall along the railway and the houses will create a rebound of the noise," he said as he laid down his newspaper.

"But every time I stop walking, the steps behind me keep going for a while."

"Yes; that's the delayed echo."

"Is there nobody behind me, then?" I trembled.

"No, I think I know the problem," dad said. "It's the tackets in your boots."

"Is that all it is?" I asked with joyful relief. "Could you put rubber soles on my boots, dad? Would that stop it?"

"Yes, I think so."

* * *

"That's a lot better. Didn't hear any footsteps behind me tonight." But I still wasn't convinced, I confessed to mum.

"Why are you so scared? Are you still worried about that man?" mum asked.

"Yes, I think so."

I was referring to a scare I had a few weeks earlier when the railway gates were closed and the small wicket locked, and I was forced to walk across the bridge. Again, I was walking home from Scouts and – just as I was about to descend the steps – a man wearing a long dark coat appeared from the direction of the beach. His head was entirely wrapped in a white bandage, with tiny spaces for his eyes and nose. The wind was howling and the sea was roaring. I stood still and wanted to go back, but knew there was nowhere to go. I glanced at the window of the signal box seeking help, but couldn't see the signalman. I remember making a decision to take what I thought was the only action; to walk on down the steps. My stomach was churning and my head was reeling; I felt as if I might be walking towards my executioner. We passed each other half-way without any communication. To this day I can't think what could have been wrong with the man, but on those dark, gas-lit nights I was convinced he was following me. The removal of tackets did help – but not a lot.

* * *

One evening I had a delivery to the company director's home at Barry. The wind was blowing from the west, and it was raining heavily. By the time I got the box out of the basket and held it with my right arm while I undid the gate latch, the groceries were wet. I'd had to leave the sack over another order in my basket. There was no light to be seen when I rang the bell, but the noise of wind in the trees drowned out any confirmation that it had worked. I stood there, trying to use my cape as a shield over the groceries. Someone switched on the hall light. Could it be Mr Stewart – and am I about to hand over soggy bags and then be sacked?

I stood petrified.

"Hello, Mrs Stewart. I'm sorry your things are a bit wet," I said nervously, but hugely relieved it wasn't her husband who answered the door.

"Oh, it's a dreadful night Robert," she said sympathetically as I passed over the box.

She never asked me to carry boxes to her kitchen like some ladies did, and I always imagined that was because her husband didn't want me seeing inside their house.

"There you are Robert," she said as she returned the wet box. "I'll just dry things out."

As I walked hurriedly back to her front gate to check the state of the other box for Mrs Evans who lived further along the village, I consoled myself with two thoughts. One was that some apparently poorer people always routinely gave generous tips even when the weather was good, while this delivery for a director was seen as an internal business delivery even on very uncomfortable days. I wasn't critical; it was quite simple – this was a view of my customer which I happily accepted. I recalled Freddie's words – don't expect a tip. My other thought was that if Mr Stewart heard about wet goods, he may not be so understanding as his wife. Time would tell. This was another worry, rather like the Mrs McDonald windy day, and I was convinced Mrs Stewart – who I thought was a genuinely friendly person – would probably say something to the boss.

My theory about tips was confirmed when I delivered groceries to Mrs Evans. Her box was damp and the bag of biscuits on top looked as if was about to burst, but nevertheless she gave me a florin. What was even better, it was handed over by her lovely wee daughter Ellie.

Nice wee lass, but too young for me!

On my way back to the shop with the wind behind me, I passed the bungalow beside Barry school. Mum had told me that was where I was born. Mum and dad had rented part of the house when dad worked at Barry railway station, which was only five minutes away by bicycle. When I arrived home quite wet, mum draped all my clothes in front of the coal fire.

"Goodness me! How far did you have to travel tonight?" she said as she adjusted the drying screen.

"Around the town, and a long run out to Barry."

"No wonder you're so wet, cycling into the wind," she said with concern.

"It was alright. I had a chance to see the bungalow as I passed," I said as I wriggled my blue toes in front of the fire.

"Oh, you surely can't remember anything about that! You were too young."

"I can remember crawling along a polished wood floor."

"Surely not, Robert. You weren't even two years old when we left the bungalow and moved to Annfield Cottage in Barry Road," she said incredulously.

"But I remember seeing little brown mats at each door in a long corridor."

"My goodness, yes. We did have brown mats. I can't believe you remember all that."

* * *

The pattern of my life in the shop developed. Seasonal changes introduced appropriate products. Salad and cold meat sales diminished, and soups and stews became noticeable in displays and customers' orders. Icy roads and snow brought new challenges and, when I returned to the shop, staff would give me supportive motherly-like comments. The temperature suddenly plummeted one evening and black ice formed, but deceptively the roads appeared wet. My dad had warned me about disguised ice. Steering the bike became tricky on the treacherous surface, and turning a corner into Maule Street I found my friend Jock lying under his bike with boxes scattered around him. Knowing that it could be me in that predicament, I stopped to help.

"Why are you lying down there, Jock? Are you feeling tired?" I said jokingly as I carefully braked.

"Very funny, Robbie," Jock said as he tried unsuccessfully to extricate himself from under his bike. I gingerly got off my own bike and propped it against a nearby wall, then – with my feet slipping in all directions – lifted his bike off him.

"Are you hurt, Jock?" I enquired as I leaned his bike against a hedge.

"Hurt my elbows and knees," he groaned while grimacing in pain as he tried to stand up. I started to gather the spilled groceries, and put them into his now damaged cardboard box.

"Just as well your groceries were all well wrapped, and you'd no bottles of wine in this order," I said, trying to give him some comfort.

"You see, Robbie, that's what I always tell you. We sell only quality goods – all in packets."

I knew Jock was trying to make another one of his comments about my cheap bulk products, but I couldn't help adding: "Just as well all your stuff's in quality packets, but what you really need is a quality driver on the bike!"

"Away you go!" he said as he rubbed his knees.

"There you are, Jock. All sorted," I said, putting the crumpled box into his wicker basket.

"Thanks, Robbie," he replied in a loud whisper as he tried to conceal – or exaggerate – the pain.

Once I had safely negotiated my way back to the shop, I met Cathie while she was having a late tea break.

"My goodness, Robert! You look frozen. Come and have some tea and warm yourself at the fire," she said sympathetically, adding: "I'll switch on another bar."

There was a feeling of heroism to return caked in sleet or snow or from treacherous roads and be greeted as if I'd been on some dangerous mission, which in my world I certainly felt as though I had been. While I was eating my meal that evening, I told mum of my encounter with Jock.

"My goodness! That was an awful thing to happen. Did you manage alright?" she asked as she washed a pot in the sink.

"Yes, I was fine," I replied, trying to reassure her.

"What a shame! Poor Jock," she added with genuine concern.

"Were you scared on the ice?" my sister Isobel enquired.

"I was, a little bit. But I went very slowly round corners. I think Jock went too fast," I explained, adding: "My only problem was that my legs were blue with cold."

"Oh dear, that was a shame," said mum as she took away my empty plate.

"Mum, you know Charlie – the message laddie at Johnstone's Stores? well his mum is promising him longers now that winter's coming in. Please, can I get a pair?" I asked, then held my breath – taking the opportunity to convince mum I needed long trousers.

"Well, wait and see what I can do."

* * *

"Here, try these on for size. I got them on 'appro'[1] from the Co-op," said mum as she handed me a pair of trousers a week later. "They're made of serge material, so they'll be warm for you. But if they don't fit, I'll return them."

---

[1] Co-op members were permitted to buy on credit while an item could be tried on at home, i.e. 'on approval'.

"Jings, thanks mum! They fit perfectly!" I said excitedly. I tried them on and attempted to conceal the fact they were too wide, although I was sure mum knew they didn't fit exactly.

"Well, that's fine. I'll pay for them tomorrow," she said happily.

Feeling slightly guilty about telling mum her purchase for me was perfect, I went to her bedroom and looked in the mirror, trying to convince myself they were ideal. I'd been waiting ages for longers, and I was desperate to turn up at school in them after the holiday. At long last I would wear longers and be like most of the boys in my class. The girls might notice too!

"Now you've got your long trousers, would you cycle along to Mrs Keith and return a book she lent me please?" mum said to me as I day-dreamed of my entry into the classroom and wondered how I was to keep my trousers free of oil from my bike.

"Here, take these. They're spares – you can have them," dad added, having witnessed my transformation.

I couldn't believe it: longers and bicycle clips, all in one evening! I thanked dad and off I went, feeling grown-up in my new trousers. It had started to rain and my waterproofs were in the shop, so my new trousers had an early christening.

"You can't sit around in those wet trousers all evening," mum said when I returned and sat down beside the fire.

Reluctantly, I had to go to my bedroom and change. When I took off my trousers they were so thick and wet they stood upright like a pair of black pipes, but I didn't care – I was now in 'longers' and kitted out with clips!

I was up earlier than usual next morning and off to work. As I was pulling down the shades, who should cycle past but Jock in his usual shorts.

Yes! Longers before Jock! I thought.

"Funny coincidence," he said. "My mum has ordered a pair of best tweed trousers for me, and they'll be better quality than yours. I'm going to get a nice shade of dark green. They'll be here next week."

"Will that be from her best quality shopping catalogue?" I teased.

"The wee laddie's looking right dandy the night," said the boss as I returned to the back shop after a delivery, feeling quite grown up and decidedly more comfortable. I didn't know what to say, so I just laughed – and because he was heard by Cathie and Izzie, I felt my face blush.

"Go, Go, greasy grocer go!" he said as he raised his voice and dashed off into the back store.

My skills broadened, and skinning a cheese was a fresh challenge. New Zealand red cheddar cheeses – each weighing fifty-six pounds – came in wooden crates containing two. Each cheese was drum-shaped and reminded me of my Montrose granny's pouffé which sits in front of her settee and where grandad rested his feet. Like the dates, tools were required to unpack. As with New Zealand butter, the trade name was 'Fernleaf'. Each cheese was wrapped in a waxed muslin covering. Since being made, crated and shipped, the wax on some cheeses had dried. A great deal of patience was needed to peel off the cloth, sometimes the thickness of a postage stamp. Skinning was essential, as wires were unable to cut through the cheese. It became quite common for the boss to say "skin that cheese now, Robert" as he rushed past me in his characteristic way, usually adding his strange but now-familiar chant. A small piece of cheese at home smelled like cheese, but a whole cheese had an even stronger aroma with the added mouldy, musty smell of the wrapper. Sometimes the skin of a cheese would be sweaty. I never knew why, but I imagined it must have been caused by storage conditions.

Another time-consuming task was dealing with sugar, which was made from beet in Cupar, Fife, and delivered in jute sacks – each weighing two hundredweights. It was sold in one pound or two pound thick brown paper bags. The procedure was to fill twenty bags to just under the required weight, and then put each bag back on the scale and trickle in some sugar until the scale weight began to lift. When the batch was accurately weighed, each bag was then tied with thin white string. It sold quickly, so I always had to have an eye to top up stocks. Dot trained me how to guess the weight then trickle in sugar to reach the accurate weight and talked me through how to tie the bags. "First, Robert, get the Camp Coffee tin box containing the ball of string beside you, and make sure that the string is already threaded through the wee hole in the top," she instructed, moving the box (about the size of half a brick) towards her and pointing to the hole.

I watched Dot carefully fold the lugs of the bag, place the bag upside down over a length of string laid out in a line on the bench, then tie the special slip-knot at the bottom of the bag. "Now remember, the next trick is to hold the bag in one hand and then cut the string on the razor gadget on top of the tin."

"I'll never manage this, Dot," I said despondently. It'll take me years to master."

With Dot's help I persevered, and eventually felt proud of myself when I built up quite a good speed of filling and weighing. But it took longer to tie the string around the bags.

I was devastated when my new skill became immediately redundant, because the company started to receive sugar prepacked in paper parcels, each containing fourteen two pound bags.

It was a shame to lose the unique blended aroma of the sugar and the jute bag. To lose the skill of tying the string on to the upturned bag without spilling sugar was bad enough, but what was more disappointing was that I had begun to master the knack of judging the weight before I put a bag on the scales. I was hugely disappointed, but I suppose I was witnessing progress and could see how this one simple change would save many hours of staff time.

Thinking back to the box which contained the ball of string, I began to wonder why coffee was called Camp. One afternoon I asked Dot. "Look at the picture on the tin," she said. "It's a soldier in a camp in Africa, being served coffee by a native. It looks like a scene from the last century or before."

"What's so special about Camp Coffee, Dot?"

"Ah, well, that's why it's so unique – because the coffee is an essence sold in bottles. You just need to add hot water. That would be a lot easier than roasting and grinding beans while camping in the middle of a jungle somewhere."

"That's a clever idea, Dot," I said. "I wonder who invented the essence?"

"I don't know, but you see – there's always a reason behind a product."

As I cycled home that evening, I marvelled at what Dot had said and wondered if I could think of a new product someday.

Once I learned the stock locations, moving into the front shop to fill shelves became a more comfortable experience, but I still kept clear of the serving area.

"Always sell old stock first, Robert," the boss said every time he dashed past while I was replenishing products. "Why is that, do you think?"

"Oh, is it to stop customer complaints?" I said hesitantly.

"You're nearly right. It's called stock rotation." Then he sped off, chanting his usual words.

I made a mental note to ask Jock Brown if he rotated his high-quality products.

"Come and help me to face up the canned fruits," Isobel asked me one day when all my other jobs had been done.

"What does face up mean?" I enquired.

"Don't push stock to the back of the shelf unless we're stocktaking. Always bring the cans or packets to the front. That way the shop looks full and better presented."

"Ah! Is that why the shop always looks full?"

She showed me how to do that with cans of sliced peaches with the brand name Libby's. After we did the facing up, Izzie selected some cans from around the shop and told me about the names of can sizes by laying out a sample of each size. The smallest can of Heinz baked beans was what she called a picnic size. Next, she pointed to a can of soup and told me that was an A1 which, she said, always contained around sixteen ounces in weight. The largest can of Peaches was called an A 2.5.

It was more for me to think about. Imagine that! All the time I'd been delivering cans, I had no idea they had names.

A few more testing teasers for Jock whenever we next met.

CHAPTER 6

Window Displays and Spiders, or "Have You Checked for Maggots?"

November 1953

"**N**O! I'm not touching them!" screamed Izzy as she, with a backward glance at a Fyffes wooden banana box – and to the alarm of customers – ran to the back shop.

"What's wrong?" asked the boss in amazement as he emerged from his office.

"There's a huge spider in that box. I'm not touching those bananas!" Izzy exclaimed, her face drained with shock.

"Dearie me, Isobel. It'll not kill you!" the boss said with a wicked grin. "Robert! Stop cleaning these brass weights. Go and catch it in an empty jam jar," he instructed with mock annoyance as I dashed off to get a jar from the back store.

"That's the first time that's happened to me," I heard Izzy – now in a state of terror – tell the boss.

When I reached the front shop and approached the four foot long box, I sensed all business at the counter had ceased and customers were becoming excited about Izzy's alleged find. I knelt beside the box – which in my mind now took on the appearance of a coffin – and searched for the alleged offending eight-legged arachnid.

"Watch it's no' a giant Jamaican spider like the one I read aboot in the *Evening Tele*!" a customer called out, just as my doubts began to creep in.

"Aye, it was as big as a man's hand!" added another customer with no thought of my mental state.

Despite my fears, I secretly hoped I would find the biggest one in the country and the shop would get a mention in the newspaper, but I quickly abandoned that notion when I started to move closer to the box. With great care and close inspection I removed the bananas and picked out pieces of the straw bed in which they had been packed. At this point my fears began to build up, but now – being in the limelight – I had no choice but to continue. I began to imagine the cluster of customers saw me as something akin to a bomb disposal expert, and I sweated. I didn't want to be a dead hero. To my great relief, a spider that would fit into a matchbox ran to a corner of the box and luckily I managed with my first

Isobel and the Scary Spider

78

attempt to cup the jar over it. With the immigrant invader safely in a jar – and with the lid on – I held it up for all to see. Customers gathered around and Isobel reappeared to inspect the dreaded spider.

"It's no' so big as the ane they found in Dundee!" remarked one woman.

"You see, Isobel? It's just a wee one," said the boss as he called out from behind the cluster of customers. "Robert, empty the box and put all the straw in the waste bin."

I could tell he was agitated, and really wanted the crowd of customers and staff to get back to normal business. I did as he asked, but didn't assume there had been only one spider.

"All straw now dumped and no more spiders," I reported to the boss after a few minutes.

I had heard stories about spiders in boxes, and wasn't at all certain they were safe. The boss had previously told me that bananas were despatched green from their country of origin, partially ripened on ship, and then stored in warm conditions to ripen in a wholesaler's warehouse in straw-lined wooden boxes. Like bottles, banana containers were returnable, and in those days a box was worth a refund of ten shillings and sixpence.

"The warm conditions would bring the spiders out of hibernation," he told me quietly later.

A bunch of, say, ten or twelve bananas was called a hand, and these were laid neatly in a box on a bed of straw to stop bruising during transport. Isobel had been removing hands to make a display at the fruit counter when her horror moment occurred.

"In future, Izzy, just ask me to check the box before you start," I said heroically.

"Thanks, Robert," she replied with seeming reassurance.

* * *

By now I had a good knowledge of my round. On my travels I found that I could predict the smell of a house before I arrived. Each house had a different odour, which I could usually foretell. Sometimes it was a reeky smell, if someone smoked inside the house. Some homes, week after week, always had the same cooking smell. I could eventually predict if a customer had fish every Thursday, or perhaps a fried meal every Wednesday. I realised my house too would also have a smell. I didn't discuss my thoughts with anyone, but it was interesting to observe.

I was also able to study the various attitudes of customers and their mannerisms, and I tried to put them into categories: cheery, grumpy, worried, friendly, smiling, unfriendly, monosyllabic, and so on. I found that I could also tell in advance the state of dress people would wear: tidy, untidy, bright, dull, fresh and clean, or even which customers were likely to appear in pyjamas or nightgowns!

One delivery that I couldn't get to quickly enough was to Mrs Smith, because each time I approached the house her daughter Jenny was there at the door. I don't know how she did it but, as soon as I'd knocked on the door, Jenny was immediately there to open it. There were occasions when, from the end of the street, I would see her waiting at her door. I would pass the box to Jenny, and she would come back with my tip. She had been in my class, but she went on to Arbroath High School. I probably stared at Jenny so much I didn't have time to notice smells and mannerisms at her house, but funnily enough I can remember her blue eyes.

* * *

The shop was double fronted, which meant it had two windows measuring around nine feet square. While working during my holidays, I found that on Mondays products in each were removed, the bases cleaned and inside plate glass polished. By evening, the boss had put in new displays. He used specially-printed price tickets for some products, so I guessed he was told by head office which stock to display. Provisions filled the window on the left of the entrance. Eggs and cooked meats took up most space, while bacon was displayed along the back on a chest-high marble shelf. For easy access, bacon and meat-slicing machines were located at the end of the counter nearest the window. Cans of meats, soups or vegetables were stacked in towers or pyramids at each side of the window.

One of the first things I learned about bacon was that if a label described it as Ayrshire, it didn't mean it came from that county. It was a description of the style in which the pig had been butchered. This had been a puzzle for me, as I had noticed red dye stamps on some bacon skins stating Produce of Poland. The cuts had names: fore, middle, back, streaky, and gammon. We sold smoked and unsmoked bacon, and the latter – I learned – was referred to as 'green' bacon. Fores, middles and gammons were each fashioned in a long roll shape, encased in a viscose which looked like film or plastic. Sometimes two or three fores would be contained in a muslin net. The others were sold as flat, unwrapped cuts. I had some confusion about the difference between bacon and ham, and one day – while I was helping the boss to carry some bacon to the back shop – I asked him about it.

"Every cut off the side of a pig is called bacon, but if the gammon (or hind leg) is cut off and cured or smoked separately then it's a ham," he told me as he removed the muslin coat surrounding a fore.

There was also a lot to learn in recognising cooked meats for slicing, and the ones I remember were jellied veal, brisket, corned beef, and spam. It was important to know the differences between boiled shoulder, boiled gammon and boiled ham, as I had to recognise each. Jock always boasted about selling only best Belfast ham, but I had been told it didn't come from Belfast. It was simply a style of curing, but Jock didn't seem to know that. Perhaps I could tease him about that someday.

It was difficult to keep cooked meat products in good condition in summer months, and the preserving jelly in which they were canned melted and they went soft. There was no fridge, so at the end of each evening I was given the job to put each item cut-face down on a marble slab and cover it with muslin. The boss asked me to keep an eye open for fly larvae. Inevitably there was grease everywhere on the floor of the fridge and behind the counter. When I opened cans of such greasy meats my hands were covered in sticky grease. It didn't take me long to see where the boss's appropriate chant came from.

"Have you checked for maggots?" he would regularly ask as he dashed along at great speed.

Occasionally I did, usually in the folds of bacon when I had to scrape them off then pour boiling water over them and dispose down the drain. The boss once asked me to remove part of the can opening device which was fitted to the edge of a bench in the back store. It was a gadget called a "Bonzer", whereby any large can containing cold meat for slicing was punctured by a blade. A handle was then bent over and turned, making it very efficient to open large numbers of cans. The part I had to remove was the base, which had been cracked for quite some time. On doing so I found a squirming mass of maggots which I had to scoop up, throw in the sink, and dispose of them in the usual way. It turned my stomach to deal with them, and I always felt unclean afterwards until I washed at home. Mum would not have been impressed if I had told her I had dealt with maggots.

Butters, too, were equally difficult to keep. Grooved wooden butter pats were used to scoop portions off the blocks. Although I wasn't allowed to touch butter, I was given the job of washing the pats and the water jug they sat in all day. This was important, as it stopped butter sticking to the pats. New Zealand butter was displayed in original fifty-six pound blocks, while Danish was displayed in the half barrel style of the same weight. Each one was on a porcelain base, permanently labelled with the country of origin. Those salted butters stayed firm, but Cathie had told me that during summer unsalted Dutch nearly melted off the shelf. Whether it was meats, bacon or butter, I could see how easy it was to lose money while handling them. One day I plucked up the courage and asked the boss how he could make up for the losses.

"It's very easy to throw money down the drain if you're not careful. Provisions are a large part of our business, so the losses can be great too," he said seriously while peeling soft jelly off a six-pound boiled shoulder.

"How do you make up for the losses?" I enquired while watching the boss put what looked like a pound of greasy jelly into the bin.

"Well, you just have to be efficient with everything else you handle. But don't do what the grocer in Aberdeen was caught doing. Did you not read about it in the papers?" he said with a loud laugh.

"No, what did he do?" I replied seriously and warming to the discussion.

"Well, he was reported by a customer, or a member of his staff, for cheating and fined a lot of money: a hundred pounds, I think. But worse, he lost his customers for being a bad boy."

"How did he cheat?" I was intrigued.

"Well, boiled shoulder sells at 1/3 a quarter and boiled gammon is priced at 1/6 a quarter so, if he got a very lean shoulder, he converted it to a gammon, and if he had a very lean gammon he would roll it in fish dressing and label it a York ham priced at 2/3 for a quarter!"

"Gee whiz! He must have been daft," I blurted.

"Or desperate, because he also did the same kind of thing with tomatoes," the boss said damningly.

"How did that work?" I asked inquisitively.

"Tomatoes from Holland – that's the ones in flat trays – sell at 1 shilling a pound, and he put them into a Guernsey box and sold them for one and sixpence a pound. Then he got greedy and changed the Guernseys into Scottish baskets, selling at two and sixpence a pound."

"Wow, he must have made a fortune!" I exclaimed.

"Nobody knows how long he'd been cheating, but anyway – he's out of business now, with a bad reputation."

"Gee, what a silly thing to do," I said, finding myself criticising a grocer unknown to me.

"Well, he's paid the price in a big way," the boss remarked as he washed the grease off his hands at the sink, then walked off a great speed chanting "Go, go, greasy grocer go." I thought I saw him wink – or was it some grease in his eye? I was left thinking about his chant; was it directed at the fraudulent grocer?

Additionally, there was a 'fruit' window, where towers of canned fruits or juices were built at each side. Pyramids of fresh apples, oranges and pears were built on wooden trays laid on boards which sloped from shoulder height at the back of the window to the bottom of the glass. Depending on the season, melons, grapes or bananas were placed between each pyramid. I wasn't allowed to stand inside the window, but I was given the job of polishing apples: such as Cox's Pippins, Canadian MacIntosh reds, Granny Smiths, and Bramley cookers.

"I polished all these apples!" I couldn't help saying to my pals as I walked past the shop.

"That's cissy stuff, Robbie! Anybody could do that," the engineering-minded amongst them would reply. They were right; it was kid's stuff. But for me, I was beginning to develop a serious understanding of how best to display products with the object of improving sales.

* * *

When I arrived home for tea one evening, I had some news for mum.

"Mum, you told me that we moved from the bungalow at Barry to Annfield Cottage. Is that the white building near the corner of Barry Road and James Street?"

"Yes, that's the one."

"Well, I was near there tonight when I had to deliver a big box to a Mrs Wilson," I said while mum was serving my meal.

"Oh yes, I remember her. She was always very pleasant, and liked to know how you were all getting on," she told me as she tidied the table.

"She knew about Peem, and said she remembered when Isobel was born. She recalled you seeing me safely across the road on my way to Barry school."

"I'm sure she would. We often chatted when we met in Warren's Barry Road Stores."

"She told me about the days when the pipe bands marched past Annfield," I said.

"That's right, but you wouldn't remember that."

"Yes, I do. I can think of a lot of things that happened at Annfield."

"What kind of things?" she enquired. "But come on now; eat up your food before you tell me."

While I ate my custard and prunes, I tried to think of all the things that happened at Annfield. By now, Peem and Isobel – who had already eaten – were back at the table, waiting to hear what I had to say.

"I didn't know you went to Barry school, Robert," Isobel said as she wriggled in her chair.

"It was only for one year. I remember my teacher was Miss Bell, and there must have been about three or four classes with only twelve pupils in one room. I sat beside a lovely warm coal fire with a guard around it, and I can still smell the mixture of chalk, warm paper and coal dust in the classroom."

"A real fire in the classroom?" Isobel said disbelievingly.

"Yes, that was the best part. But the worst thing were school lunches. 'Robert Murray! You're last again to eat your lunch! Hurry up and get back out to play,' one of the school dinner ladies said to me almost every day while I carefully picked through my food. They probably wanted to get away home. Almost as bad as the food was being the only pupil to walk to school along the dusty cinder footpath when the road was flooded, forcing me to tip-toe along the top of the dry, narrow grass verge."

"Did you ever fall off the grassy bit?" asked Isobel, warming to my tales.

"Yes, once. I overbalanced and stood in water up to near my knees. It was always scary, because the fields on both sides of the road were flooded and there never seemed to be any other people or cars around."

"Tell me more," Isobel pleaded.

"It's strange, but I can still remember the new leather smell of my school bag. In those days, all I had in my bag was a reading book and one apple, and I've never forgotten the smell of that rosy red fruit."

"What else can you think of?" asked Peem.

"I remember mum saying 'I hear German bombers! We must put out all our lights,' and I can still remember the long, slow drone of the engines."

"Bombers!" cried Peem. "Real bombers, mum?"

"That's right. They were on their way to drop bombs on Clydebank and Greenock beside the River Clyde. That's how Grandad Murray came to be bombed in his house at Rossie Island, Montrose – it was Germans trying to bomb the railway bridge on their way back to base. He was lucky, but his next-door neighbour was killed."

"Tell us more," said Isobel.

"I can remember mum saying she heard the skirl of the pipes and took us to the pavement on Barry Road to watch the army pipe band marching past and wave to the soldiers."

"It must have been a horrible time living at Barry," said Isobel.

"It was wartime, and things were very scarce," mum pointed out, turning around from the sink.

"I remember the day the butcher came to take Neddy and Freddy away," I said.

"Who were they?" asked Isobel.

"They were our pet rabbits," Peem joined in.

"We were not going to be able to take them to West-haven with us, and there was a shortage of food in the town," mum explained.

"And I remember the gamekeeper coming for our ban-tam hens," I added. "Was his name Braithwaite?"

"Yes, that's right. Dad had advertised them for sale be-cause we also couldn't take them to Westhaven, but they weren't killed. The gamekeeper wanted them to sit and hatch pheasant's eggs at Panmure Estate."

"We must have had a bad life at Annfield, mum," sighed Isobel.

"It was a happy time, but the war made it difficult and when dad was out on his nightshifts it was worrying. It was a cramped, dark, one bedroom cottage. The windows were small, and dad was always busy painting and stippling all the walls to make it brighter inside. It was difficult, because we had to share an outdoor toilet with a rickety door and a sneck that didn't work properly."

"What's stippling, mum?" Peem enquired.

"It was a way of dabbing on colours of paint to make the wall look like it was wallpapered."

88

"And what's a 'sneck', mum?" asked Isobel.

"That's a hook to keep the door closed."

"Do you remember the rats and mice in the loft, Robbie?" Peem queried.

"I do, especially when we were all quiet. I can still hear the scratching and pattering noises."

"Oh, you remember that? Well that was one of the reasons I wanted to move out of the cottage," mum said.

"Tell us what else you can think of, Robert," said Isobel, who had never heard of these tales.

"No, that's enough for one night. It's time for your bed, Isobel. The McLagans are out, so you have time to practise the Sailor's Hornpipe before you get to bed."

"Just one more thing, mum. Mrs Wilson asked me if I remembered the sweetie mannie and I said yes, but I don't really know much about him."

"He came from Arbroath on the train or the bus, and walked all over the town selling in a different part every day."

The Arbroath Sweetie Man

"What did he look like?" asked Isobel.

"He was stooped over because he had a big biscuit tin across each shoulder tied with string and another smaller one hanging in front, and he carried a suitcase in each hand. Somehow he used a brolly when it rained."

"What did you buy from him, mum?"

"I didn't need to buy from him, but because he was

89

a poor hard working man doing a job in all weathers I occasionally bought a packet of tea and some biscuits. And I always bought a wee sweetie for James and Robert."

"I remember a fish wife coming to Annfield," said Peem.

"Yes, she came from Arbroath on a train and carried a wicker basket on her back held up by a broad strap across her forehead. Her fish were always fresh."

"Why did they come all that distance to sell things?" Peem asked.

"People didn't have work, so they had to try and make a job for themselves. You had to admire them. The sweetie man and the fish wife came to sell here at Westhaven too. We have always been lucky, because we had a rag and bone man who sharpened knives. And for a while, an onion Johnny came around the doors on a bike with strings of onions hanging from his handle bars. But come on now; off to bed. That's enough storytelling for one night," mum urged. "That's only five minutes left for your Sailor's Hornpipe now, Isobel."

As I lay in bed that night, I began to realise that not only was my message laddie job giving me more shop jobs to do like the boss had said, but I was learning a lot about my own history as I travelled around on my bike. In my own way, I had begun to discover a competitive edge – mainly through my banter with Jock and (I was quite sure, but couldn't prove it) because of our growth I was easily beating him with the number of boxes delivered and tips earned. Proactively, I began to boast.

"Have you seen our queues on Saturdays, spread from the counter to the pavement and along the front of the provisions window?"

"Oh yes, Robbie – but our select customers don't like to queue like that! They've got telephones! "

Staff began to discuss the approach of Christmas and their expectations of late nights, massive sales of everything, and a great increase in the number of deliveries. I sensed bigger challenges were to come my way.

CHAPTER 7

Full-Time Work at Christmas, or "Separate Your Coins Next Time!"

November 1953

NO more school holidays until Christmas and, in addition to my growing list of shop jobs, I was out on the bike, as usual. But my front tyre was giving me cause for concern: it had a slow puncture. I was reluctant to ask the boss for a repair or a new tyre so, in the absence of a shop pump, I solved the problem by using my own. When I went home one evening a week or two later, mum told me that she didn't like to see my money lying around.

"It's because my syrup can's filled to the top," I said, defending myself.

"You'll have to open a bank account," she advised strongly.

"I can't go into the Royal Bank with all these coins, mum! They won't like it."

"Well, go to the Post Office in Queen Street. Miss Black will help you," mum suggested.

Plucking up the courage one Tuesday, I rushed home from school, and then took my syrup can and cloth bag – each filled with my tips – to the Post Office. I'd never been in the building before, and my first impression was the smell of glue and ink mixed with the scent of warm paper. While standing in the queue, I gazed around at the posters and notices. One large sign, I remember, was a cartoon-type picture of a post-man in a Santa Claus outfit with a postbag over his shoulder. While I waited in line, I noticed there was only one lady be-hind the counter and concluded this must have been Miss Black. At least, that's what the name plate said. She was a plump, elderly woman, and gave me the impression of being quite grumpy. Her hair was short, black and straight. Thick, black-framed spectacles matched her uniform-style jacket. Eve-rything about Miss Black was black – including her scowl. She seemed efficient, but never smiled and had a fierce way of rubber-stamping papers. It was always four rapid, loud, almost angry stamps as she dealt with postal orders or money. I then began to hope this wasn't Miss Black – perhaps this lady was a holiday relief or just another assistant. At last my turn came, and I nervously stepped forward to the counter.

"Mum wants me to open a bank account," I said as I trembled.

"Yes, well?" Miss Black snapped.

"I've got all my money here," I continued, indicating my can and bag.

"Is your money counted?"

I shook my head. Of course, I had counted it so I knew what I had, but I was now fearful of my count being wrong. Miss Black – grunting and looking grim – held out her hand, but the can was too big to pass through the grille. She huffed and puffed.

"Give me the bag," she instructed.

I slid it under the grill. She moved to the end of the counter then unlocked a metal gate.

"Bring the can here," Miss Black commanded.

She tipped out my coins; pennies, ha'pennies, threepenny bits, silver threepences, shillings, florins, half crowns, and two shirt buttons which I'd forgotten to remove.

Miss Black sighed and groaned. Mum hadn't told me she was a tough lady. As she sorted my coins, her queue lengthened and shuffling feet behind me grew louder. I was aware that I was the cause. If I'd told her the coins were counted, I'm sure Miss Black would have checked them in any case. As she counted, my gaze fell on her jacket badge. It read "Miss A. Black" – perhaps the 'A' denotes 'All', I thought. Eventually she had what looked like a new bank book in her hand.

"Name, address?"

"Do I need to tell you my middle name?" I said quietly in case people behind me thought I was stupid.

"Of course you do." she said staring directly at me.

As she wrote something on a document she muttered "Eight pounds, twelve shillings and four pence." Then I saw her rapid movement with the rubber stamp - from ink pad to bank book and back to pad - then to her own paper record. So, that's what she does. The amount was exactly as I had counted. Opening the gate, she handed back the empty can, then barked in her gruff voice: "Separate your coins next time!"

The buttons were left on her counter, but I was too scared to ask for them. With my hand on the door handle and just about to leave, I heard Miss Black's deep sergeant major's voice. "Here, you'd better take these!" she said, emphasising 'these'. The buttons.

Once home, I proudly showed mum my new bank book before asking her if she would deposit my money next time as Miss Black scared me.

"Oh, you mustn't say that about Miss Black! She is a good, church-going person with a heart of gold. She is just being very careful to do her job accurately."

I remember thinking that mum had taught me, in future, to differentiate between personality and efficiency.

* * *

"Are you able to work full-time over the Christmas and New Year period, Robert?" the boss asked me one evening in his characteristic urgent style.

I had been hoping for this request. The prospect of getting more involved in the day-to-day action and discovering the buzz of Christmas trading, along with the attraction of more pay and tips, was too much to miss.

"Yes, I'll be here," I replied enthusiastically.

"Well done! It'll be a good greasy grocer experience for you. Go, go, greasy grocer go!" he chanted as he zoomed off with a large, freshly-cut wedge of cheese in each hand.

* * *

"I don't want to miss out on this one," said the boss in a serious tone. "It's a new delivery to Anderson Grice foundry canteen before nine o'clock in the morning. It's a big order of bacon, eggs and sugar, and it starts on Monday next week."

"That's great," I said enthusiastically.

"Can you be here at 8.30 Monday morning?" I sensed he was hesitant, perhaps half expecting me to decline.

"Yes, but will I get back in time for school?" I queried, knowing it was a long trip to the west end of town and near the railway line.

"You'll just have to," he replied rather unsympathetically.

"Well, alright then," I said, realising that the boss needed help but at the same time feeling unconvinced about the time available to do the run.

I didn't like the sound of it, and the boss hadn't mentioned any extra pay. When I turned up at half-past eight, the ladies weren't ready – the shop blinds were still down, and the boss was busy slicing bacon for the order. I was dismayed, but felt I couldn't walk away. By 8.45 the order was prepared and I was off like a rocket, noticing as I passed that nearly all my school pals were already in the playground. The round trip would take about fifteen minutes, and I knew I was in for trouble because – on that first Monday – I had to face the usual strong west wind, which delayed me. On the return leg I could see the usual cluster of pals clamouring at the seniors' door to be allowed to ring the bell, and I still had to park the message bike and cycle to the bike shed! As I left the shop the school bell stopped ringing, and though I'll never know how, I somehow managed to be in the classroom on time. This agonising delivery became a regular feature of my Monday morning. I don't think the boss ever knew how nerve-wracking it was for me.

* * *

Tuesday evenings were always different, as it was half day closing and I had no deliveries. It was an evening for an earlier tea, and extra time to do homework prior to setting off for my much-awaited Scout evening with Peem, who was now in the same troop. On one Tuesday in late November, mum wasn't around when I arrived home from school.

"You're going to have an earlier tea tonight," dad said when Peem and I appeared.

"Why? Where's mum?" we both said, almost in unison.

"She's in her bed," he told us as he shakily put a plate of sandwiches down on the kitchen table.

"What's wrong? Is she ill?" I asked worriedly.

"No, she'll be alright. The nurse will be here soon," he said in a tone of unconvincing calm.

Peem and I looked at each other as we sat down at the table. We ate in silence and wondered what was going on. Dad disappeared now and again and, after we'd had our custard and jelly, we put our dishes beside the sink.

Dad reappeared. "Here's money to you both. You'll need to go to the pictures tonight," he said in an unfamiliar and nervous voice as he put down a half crown on the table.

Dad, giving us money to go to the cinema? This was an unheard-of event, and Peem and I looked at each other in amazement. At that moment there was a knock on the door.

"Oh yes, nurse, she's through here," I heard dad say, and I caught a glimpse of a lady in a dark blue coat carrying a large brown leather case on her way – I assumed – to mum's bedroom.

"Can we go through to see mum?" I asked, fully expecting dad to say no. I wasn't wrong.

"Dad, we go to Scouts tonight. This is Tuesday," I said, including Peem in my thoughts as I pushed dad's money across the table towards him.

Dad looked confused. "Oh, alright then. Off you go and get changed," he said with some more composure.

While Peem and I were putting on our Scout uniform, I became aware of a Dettol-like smell in the house. And then I heard it: a baby's cry! It was a huge shock, but at the same time a relief. Of course, it was mum's baby.

"Thank goodness she's not ill at all!" I said to Peem with great relief.

We stayed out of sight in our room for a while in some trepidation, and aware of hurried footsteps to and from mum's room. Eventually we returned to the living room to find dad apparently deep in thought and staring out of the window.

"Can we see the baby?" Peem asked him.

"What's that?" he said, turning his head towards us. Peem repeated the question. "No, nobody's allowed in there yet. You have a wee sister, but you have to go now. Your mum's sleeping."

After all those months of embarrassment and wonder, it had finally happened. I remember the relief: mum wasn't ill at all! But when I heard dad say she was sleeping, I still worried. I'd seen films where a mother dies when a baby is born. Would this happen to mum?

On our way to Scouts, Peem and I spoke openly for the first time together about the worries and feelings we'd had about mum's big tummy, and discovered we had both had similar silent concerns about mum all those months. When I arrived at the Scout hut, I had an urge to tell Skipper about my news. My mind went back to the time I helped to carry mum's bag across the field at my camp. Somehow, I wanted my Scout master to know the event had happened and that mum wasn't just fat after all.

"I got a wee sister tonight, Skipper," I said proudly.

"Oh, did you? Well, congratulations," he responded casually with a smile.

He took the news all in his stride, and I had a calm, relaxed feeling that all my embarrassment had been unnecessary. I felt the arrival of my wee sister had made the situation clean, respectable and acceptable. When we arrived home that evening, dad said we could see mum and the baby. We went to her room, and I was not quite sure what to expect. Mum was propped up in bed, and the baby was asleep in a cot – which, like the baby, seemed to have miraculously appeared. Isobel was sitting on a chair, just staring at the infant. Dad hovered in the background.

"You've got a wee sister!" said mum with a huge smile, and looking the happiest I'd ever seen.

That was the scene I'll always remember: dad, Peem and me standing at the bottom of the bed, and Isobel absorbed by the tiny pink, breathing bundle in the cot. I stood there mesmerised, thinking: *So that's the wee thing that was in mum's tum when she came to visit me at camp in the summer.*

"Say hello to Jean," mum said.

We all said hello in unison, and I remember feeling pride in being the big brother of such a wee baby. When I went into the shop on Wednesday, I was by then so relieved that mum was well and the baby wasn't screaming, I announced to the boss that I had a baby sister. He then went around chanting "the greasy grocer's now a dad" so that all the staff heard. It was his humorous way of congratulating me. The ladies asked me questions about names, the baby's

weight, and other questions for which I didn't have answers –
apart from the name. Once my sister had arrived, I had a
strange feeling of being more adult and somehow had a sense
of responsibility. As the days passed, baby Jean's existence
became an accepted part of my life.

* * *

Seasonal stock began to arrive, and one day the boss announced: "Time for new displays". Then he launched into his
chirpy "Go, go, greasy grocer go" chant. It was then I began
to suspect why he repeated the slogan so often: I sensed that
it was because he enjoyed his work so much. He was looking
forward to Christmas! It was his enthusiasm about trading
and selling that seemed to switch him on. I had a feeling the
shop ladies thought he was rather strange, but I saw it as his
positive humour to 'rally his troops' and keep morale high –
possibly including his own.

   Products in the provisions window remained almost
the same, but the fruit window was filled with trays containing cake ingredients such as currants, raisins, cut mixed peel,
dried coconut, glacé cherries and flour replaced fresh fruit. Of
course, I realised that customers like my mum would be baking Christmas cakes. I had never given it thought, but now I
was seeing things from a shop point of view. In places where I
had not previously seen stock, there were bold displays of
Christmas boxes of chocolates and biscuits with colourful designs and pictures. One counter on which sweets were usually
displayed was now given over to fruit cakes. I began to understand the cake world; Madeira, Genoa, cherry, sultana and
Dundee cakes were wrapped in bright wrappers with festive
designs, and were on sale in two or four pound pieces. Early

one evening, the boss asked me to bring down from the loft all the large cardboard egg boxes and open them up. They were the boxes in which thirty dozen eggs on papier maché trays were delivered. But now they seemed light, and I wondered why. Undoing the string and opening the bulky containers I found packets of Christmas crackers. Within a minute the boss was beside me.

"Now, Robert, this is last year's stock. We must sell these first. What do we call it?" he asked as he began removing the boxes of crackers.

"Oh! Is that stock rotation?" I replied instantly.

"Exactly," he said briskly.

At first I thought it was a bit odd, but then realised that crackers would not have deteriorated in a year. Yet I couldn't help thinking yet again that the boss had every penny counted. I made a mental note to ask Jock Brown about his crackers.

Customers, I noticed, were buying boxes of Christmas chocolates, biscuits and cakes well in advance, and having them labelled with their names and stored in the back shop. Boxes were decorated with a variety of scenes and designs, and I could see why they were so desirable. They were almost art forms, and highly desired gifts to family and friends. I asked Cathie why customers seemed desperate to buy these items.

"It's because they want to make sure they get what they want, but also it avoids a big spend all at once. They like to have them laid by, but not at home," she explained.

One day I overheard a customer asking the boss if more cakes were to be delivered from the company warehouse, and his clear reply was that no more cakes would be forthcoming. Stock availability must have been limited, and I then understood customers' anxieties. Such early buying built up gradually in the days leading up to the festive period, and I was excited and somewhat daunted to see the volume of deliveries would be considerable when added to the routine orders.

What had the biggest impact on everything was when Christmas and New Year dates fell. That determined how many days the shop would be closed. This would result in a change in buying patterns, and established how long a holiday break staff would enjoy. Some customers seemed to stockpile goods at home, and mid-week days became busier. I couldn't work full time until the school holiday began, and this resulted in an increase of bigger orders to be delivered in the two-hour evening period. It became quite hectic, and when I arrived in from school it was quite alarming to see the floor packed solidly with boxes with an overflow into the passage leading to the back shop. Hardly a day passed when there wasn't a delivery to a new customer. It was shaping up to be an exhausting Christmas.

* * *

"The Taylors have written to ask if they can stay for two weeks' holiday next year," mum said one evening at teatime. "Mrs Taylor says Charles hasn't stopped talking about fishing on the rocks with Robert, and can't wait to come back."

"Will there be space for them now that Jean is here?" I asked.

"Oh yes. Isobel wants two weeks' holiday with Granny at Woodside."

"Mr Taylor's sister and family want to come for two weeks too, as soon as the Taylors go. They're called the Christies, and they live in Grangemouth. They have a young boy and girl, and they say they will be happy to be in one room too."

"Jings! It'll be a busy time," said Peem.

I remember thinking how crowded the house would be again, like last time, although everybody seemed to fit in very well. But with baby Jean here now, it may well be more difficult. I guessed mum and dad found the extra income helpful, so I was happy for it to happen, and the fact that the Taylors wanted to return made me feel that our modest home must have had some appeal. Mum's cooking and baking may have had something to do with it.

One evening, dad looked up from the *Courier and Advertiser* he was reading to announce that the Carnoustie Coastguards would no longer carry out shipwreck rescue practice. "Thank goodness for that!" said mum as she continued knitting the pink jacket she had said was for Jean.

"Aye, we don't want another fiasco like last time," dad said in a serious tone.

He was referring to the evening when the full-time resident Coastguards, based at Westhaven and comprised of ex-Naval servicemen, held their annual rescue practice. I remember every detail so clearly, and looking back it was like a Navy version of *Dad's Army*. The concept was that if a ship had floundered on the rocks, the idea would be to set up a breeches buoy – a sort of sit-in lifebelt – to bring stricken sailors ashore. There was a pretend ship's mast – a long post about the size of a telegraph pole, with steps nailed on – which was permanently positioned at the ballaster. A rocket with a line attached was then fired across the pretend mast, and a coastguard climbed up the pole and securely fastened the line. A breeches buoy was then relayed from the shore to the pretend vessel so that personnel could be evacuated. The only problem was that the practice didn't get as far as it had previously. There had been such fiddling delays that the tide had gone back and the rocket, when fired, hit rocks and ricocheted back onto the land. Quite dangerously, it whizzed and spluttered its way back across the ballaster, eventually reaching the main road running through Westhaven where it clattered its way along the road and embedded itself in Mrs Bisset's thick hedge. All the 'Coasties', as we called them – complete in Navy uniform – came running like the Keystone Cops to grapple with the fiery beast. Mum had been standing beside the hedge watching the practice from a long way off, and was chased by the spitting cobra. There was great alarm amongst the Coasties, and somehow the story found its way into the following week's *Sunday Post*.

"No, we won't see any more stories about mum in the papers next year," he said with a laugh.

"I know! I could have been killed that night," mum reflected, putting down her knitting and looking up to the ceiling as she seemingly recalled her nightmare moment.

In today's world I'm sure somebody would have made a legal claim for damages of some sort.

CHAPTER 8

A Different Christmas, or "Headless Chickens!"

December 1953

"THE police want you to walk across the bridge on Saturday night," dad said one Monday evening.

"What, just me?"

"No, no. You and some of your pals. They'll be watching both sides of the bridge from a distance and will be ready to help."

My friends and I had been telling our parents for some time that a strange man had been speaking to them and motioning them to follow him as they were crossing the 'Smoky Brig'. I had seen a man, but he had never been close to me and hadn't said anything. It was a dark, shadowy wooden bridge with a long, narrow, badly-lit path between bushes which you had to walk through to reach it. When we crossed over on dark nights on our way home from swimming lessons at Arbroath Baths we ran in a group, but alone it was frightening –

especially when the wind howled through the slats of the bridge. We always feared there was somebody hiding in the bushes.

"The police will be there at seven o'clock. You won't see them, but you just have to walk over and they'll watch what happens. They just want to get a description of the man, and if he speaks to you they'll interview him," dad explained.

We gossiped all week about the impending horror of what seemed like a police trap, and by Saturday the testing moment had turned into a huge drama. We started to walk as requested along Tayside Street with the intention of crossing the bridge, but one by one we stopped and turned for home. Jim, to our horror, carried on over the bridge and didn't come back for what seemed an age. There were many theories about could have befallen him, but eventually he returned with a broad grin.

"Och, there was nothing to it. When I crossed over I kept walking, and a bobby stopped me and asked questions. Then he said: 'Just go back over – there's nothing to worry about tonight'."

We all stood amazed at Jim's bravery. Nothing more was ever said about the danger, but none of us crossed the 'Smoky Brig' alone again.

* * *

"Now, Robert, here's another job. I need more space to store Christmas stock, so bring from the loft all the empty tomato boxes. Freddie's coming to take them away," said the boss with some urgency as he rushed in to the back store.

"Freddie, the message boy? Is he coming back?" I queried with surprise while washing enamelled meat trays.

"No, not him. Freddie Tennant; the well-known boxer. Have you not heard of him?"

"No, I haven't."

"Well, he was a great fly-weight winner from Dundee. A clever wee boxer for many years."

I couldn't help thinking about Freddie and the humorous yet sad twist of a boxer now collecting boxes. How could he make a living with tomato boxes, and how good a boxer had he been?

"Now, here's what to do. Separate the Dutch, Guernsey and Scottish baskets, and stack them inside the back door. Let me know how many we have of each."

The boss explained that flat trays with high triangle bits at each corner were Dutch and the woven cane baskets with a metal handle were Scottish, and that the baskets – similar in size to Scottish, but made of wood – were Guernseys. I was puzzled why they were of varied design.

"Why does each country have a different box?" I asked the boss.

"It's just by chance, the way growers developed them. But it's important for us now, because we can tell at a glance where they come from."

I didn't say anything, but I remembered the boss's story about the cheating Aberdeen grocer and I could see how easy it would be to swap tomatoes into other boxes. There were dozens of boxes, and I left a note on the boss's desk with the numbers of each.

One evening, a smiling, stocky little man with a flat nose and cauliflower ears walked jauntily into the back shop. Unmistakably, this must have been the great Freddie Tennant. His appearance indicated that he must have taken some punishment. What a shame. He was a courteous, friendly man.

"Mr Stewart? Mr Tennant's here!" I called to the boss, who was inside his office.

They seemed to know each other well, and I heard them discuss the number of boxes and how much money the boss would get. It wasn't much. No more than a farthing or two for each. It was another example of the boss looking after every penny. The boxes had been saved during the last tomato season, and it took some time to help Freddie load them on to his rusty vehicle. I wanted to ask him what he would do with them, but I thought it was too nosey to ask.

The tempo of festive trade preparation increased. My full-time work started, and it was my first time to witness the hectic period blossoming. Long queues in the shop became a daily occurrence. Late opening hours meant I couldn't get home until seven or eight o'clock. More and bigger orders to deliver, happily accompanied by tips to match. I had never had so much money in my pockets and, although I still saved in my syrup can, I was now able to think what to buy mum and dad for Christmas. Gloves seemed to be the best practical gift, and I decided to steal some time to pop into the Co-op to buy them. One evening Jock cycled past me on his bike, and I could hear the clinking of bottles in his basket.

"Can't stop, Robbie! Wines and spirits flying off the shelves!" Jock called to me as he cycled past.

"Hope it's all best quality, Jock!" I replied.

I'd no time to stop either, but I was sure that he would find time later to tell me about his high-quality cheese and wines and how many bottles he'd sold. Meanwhile, I was gathering stories of massive sales of biscuits, cakes and crackers. On those winter evenings when the orders grew both in size and number, I was glad to get home and relax for a while in front of a warm coal fire. I didn't know how she did it, but mum always had a meal ready for me no matter when I appeared – for there was no way I could tell her when I would get home.

* * *

At this time, I had a new experience which had nothing to do with deliveries or shop work. It was more nerve-wracking than that. Accompanied by Mary, a classmate, I went to my first Boy Scout dance. I walked the length of the town to her home, during which time I tried to convince myself I was sick and couldn't go as my nerves were shredded. Twice I came close to turning back, but her mum was a customer and if I let her down mum would not be happy. Small town syndrome! As I approached her home, I saw her and the family at their window – obviously waiting for me to appear. *Gee, this must be a big event for them too*, I thought. I was trembling as I knocked on the front door while carefully clutching her gift – a box of Maltesers. I have no idea why I chose those chocolate balls as a gift. In films I'd seen men giving ladies chocolates, and I can remember thinking I would look too posh or grown up to emulate some film star.

It was about a 15 minute walk to the Scout hut. I'd never walked with a girl on a date before, and I was dumb struck. While walking, I began to question why I had ever had the nerve to ask Mary in the first place. I didn't regret it, but I knew I was putting myself through a dreaded test of some kind. Mary was always smiling, had a cheery face, and once waved to me while I was on my message bike. We had happened to meet in the school corridor one day, quite by chance when no one else was around, and for some reason she smiled at me and said hello. That's when I plucked up courage to invite her.

At a street nearer the hut, we met Billy Duncan hand in hand with his girlfriend. Bill was always a chirpy, cheeky chap and talked about lassies a lot. He never seemed to have any nervousness about girls, and I started to think I should take Mary's hand – but I didn't.

Another unromantic moment occurred when someone accidentally collided with Mary and the now-opened box of Maltesers fell and chocolate balls rolled out all over the Scout hut floor. Mary, I could see, was embarrassed. But it wasn't her fault, and I blamed myself for buying a stupid gift. What a waste of my tips! But I couldn't show my disappointment. It was my first date ordeal, but Mary said she'd enjoyed the evening and I felt quite grown up despite having to abandon my black pipes and wear Scout shorts and uniform.

The party ended about half-past nine, and I walked her home and said cheerio. The evening had been daunting, but Mary said she enjoyed it – though I never asked her or any-one else to a dance again. Within myself, I knew it was too stressful, and it wasn't until I joined the church dramatic club when I was about seventeen years old that I had the confi-dence to speak to girls. Somehow being in a play and deliver-ing lines written by someone else was easier.

* * *

Every shop in town, irrespective of size and type of business, had a Christmas window display. If I had to judge, I would have awarded first prize to Black the Butcher, whose shop was at the other end of the High Street. His windows were full of plucked chickens, geese, turkeys and wild fowl, all labelled and hanging from chrome rails. On the floor of the window was a pig's head with an orange in its mouth. I saw that head as I cycled past the shop each morning when the window lights were not on, and it looked quite ghostly. But when the shop lights went on later in the day, it was transformed into a friendly-looking face. I swear to this day that as I cycled past the pig's eyes followed me, and one appeared to wink. In my little world, and with my grandad's pigs in mind, I would have said he or she was once a happy pig and was now enjoying Christmas too – at great personal cost!

I'd never noticed such shop displays before. The whole town was buzzing, and it was exciting to be part of it.

One day I met Johnny Ross, the Co-op butchery lad who always said he was bored.

"How's it going, Johnny?"

"Bit spooky," he replied. "Headless chickens running around the back shop."

"Gee, I've heard about that. But is it true?" I asked eagerly.

"I'm telling you, it's a fact. But they dinna run very far. It gets boring after a while."

Wow! If that's boring, there must be something wrong with Johnny. I was never totally convinced about his headless bird story – perhaps it was just a butcher's tale.

* * *

It was Christmas Eve, and I vividly recall cycling along the High Street on my way home. I had never been out so late on any 24th of December. It was a frosty evening, and the road and rooftops were white. With gas street lights providing a circle of light around each lamp post and lit Christmas trees in some windows, it was like an olde worlde Christmas card scene. As I passed along the road, shops were in various stages of closing. At the jeweller's shop I saw the same old man I had seen at various times during the week, peering in at the window. He was wearing a long raincoat and a tweedy-looking bonnet. With his hands in his pockets he had been staring into the display often, and I came to the conclusion that he was a nervous man on a limited budget who couldn't make up his mind what to buy. I hoped he would decide before the shop closed.

"You're late home tonight. I was getting worried about you. What was the problem?" said mum as I finally staggered indoors.

"Well, it was what the boss wanted."

We had stayed open until the street went quiet and when the boss thought we'd served our last customer. Most shelves were now empty, and the shop looked like it had been ransacked. It had been an exhausting day, and the boss said we had to do the usual tidy up because we'll be busy when we re-open.

Mum had a roaring fire going, and a mouth-watering aroma of her freshly-baked Christmas pies drifted through the house. Dad was on late-shift, and until mum produced my meal I found his rocking chair a welcome retreat as I soaked up the cosy atmosphere and listened for a while to Bing Crosby singing 'Silent Night, Holy Night' on the radio. Quite a contrast from a busy day in a grocery shop!

"I forgot to tell you earlier, mum – the McLagans are out. I saw them walking towards the town," I told mum. This was because I knew Isobel wasn't allowed to dance when the downstairs McLagans were at home.

"Alright, Isobel. You can do your dance practice now."

"Can I do the Highland Fling first?" an overjoyed Isobel asked. She was already wearing her dancing pumps.

I relaxed and watched my wee sister getting ready for her dance classes, which would restart after Christmas.

I'd never had a Christmas Eve like it. It was a completely new experience, and a day of record tips – five pounds, seventeen shillings and sixpence. As I reflected on the marathon day, I wondered how Jock had got on – I'd seen that his shop lights were still on as I cycled home.

"Quality lights!" I'd muttered as I passed.

There was no sign of quality Jock; I guessed he must still be out on his bike delivering quality drinks as they flew off the shelves! Then I remembered that I hadn't seen him in his posh, dark green breeks yet. I made a metal note to ask him if Santa had brought them from Empire Stores, the mail order catalogue company.

Peem and I lay in bed chatting but, with excitement mounting, we couldn't sleep until very late. I can recall waking up early and trying to make out the shape of gifts stuck in the top of my stocking and around the bottom of the bed. Eventually, before anyone else was up and about, we bounded out of bed and started unwrapping. What had Santa brought? A book entitled *A Children's Guide to Knowledge*, but equally interesting was a little golf bag with a driver, three irons all hickory shafted, and a putter along with golf balls and tees. I couldn't wait, and I was off to the ballaster to swing my clubs – during which time I lost a few balls in the frosty white grass.

My gifts of gloves went down very well, especially with dad whose gloves were on their last legs – or hands. I still remember seeing his old ones, which had barely any wool on the inside of the fingers and palms. When I asked him about that, he said it was because they were worn where he gripped his handlebars. We all enjoyed a family lunch of roast chicken supplied by granny and grandad, and mum's special trifle sprinkled with hundreds and thousands.

* * *

After Christmas, I was left with a real sense of being a key player in the shop. Deliveries were essential, as most ladies would never have managed to carry their big purchases. It was all teamwork. Almost all the special stock had gone. Even the window displays had been invaded and stock removed. The boss was jubilant, and was more galvanised than usual.

My next treat was to be taken by dad, along with Peem, to the Cross in the town on Hogmanay. There must have been about two hundred people there. It was a cold wait until Rita Macbeth broke the excited chatter with her pipe tune 'Wi' a Hundred Pipers'. There was much handshaking, and then people seemed to set off in different directions. Dad told me they were off first-footing, with some clutching a dressed herring or a piece of coal as gifts and the essential bottle of whisky to share when 'first footing' friends and family.

"Why do they have a dressed herring, dad?" I asked.

"Oh, it's an ancient tradition going back to the days when the fisher folk were wishing their friends a good fishing harvest in the coming year."

"And why the coal?" Peem asked.

"Ah," said dad, "that's to wish your friend a warm house. It's where the saying 'Lang may yer lum reek' comes from."

As we stood there mesmerised by the scene – and each wearing a brown woollen balaclava, which mum had knitted for us – little did I think we would be setting off four years later to 'first foot' friends complete with a piece of coal and a herring dressed up in crepe paper.

On our first experience we, along with a few pals, walked on a cold night – immediately after midnight – almost to Barry, where I remember entering a small remote cottage heated by an enormous log fire. After a sing song we were given sandwiches and home-baked cake and black bun. We then turned back towards the town and, after a few 'first foot' visits to friends' houses, we trekked to Muirdrum village about two miles away. After some merry well-wishing, we slept on the floor of our host's living room until about 7 am when we wandered our weary way home after a round trip of almost six miles.

New Year trading had been as busy as the previous week, and I noticed that the boss cut up unsold large cakes and sold them off in small portions. He seemed to have an idea for every sales opportunity.

Several boxes of crackers were still left on display, and one day I was asked to retrieve the egg boxes, pack the crackers, and store them in the loft. Last year's stock had sold, and I hoped I'd be around to open the boxes next Christmas.

January was a quiet period, and I continued with my usual jobs. One evening the boss gathered us together as he normally did to read out price changes. He cleared his throat, then read from a piece of paper: "To all staff in Carnoustie branch. Well done everybody; you had the largest ever increase of sales in my area over the festive period. The directors have asked me to thank you all for your hard work. Signed: Mr Munro."

We each had a chance to read the note after he pinned it on the spice drawer in the back shop. The boss was grinning from ear to ear.

"Right then, Robert" he said with a smile. "There's a cheese to skin before you get home tonight." And yes, he couldn't resist his usual greasy grocer chant!

Situation normal. Skinning cheeses was nothing new. No panic. I'd survived a quick learning process since my first days on the bike in July, and now had a Christmas and New Year behind me. All the scary stories had been true.

Loads of tales to trade with Jock.

I chose this moment to tell the jubilant boss that I needed a repair to my front tyre.

"That's fine. Take the bike to Willie Clark next Monday when it's quiet, and bring me the bill."

"Phew!"

CHAPTER 9

A Big Step Forward, or "Munro's on His Way"

Early 1954

IT was a Sunday sometime in February, and about three inches of snow had fallen since early forenoon. As we walked across the 'Steenie Brig' on our way home from church, we could see that it was in perfect condition for our favourite winter sport.

"Can we go sledging?" asked Peem.

I knew the answer before it came from dad.

"No, you can't. You'll have your lunch first, then do your school homework before you get out."

Both Peem and I could hardly contain our frustration, for we knew it was only a matter of time before the town council lorry would arrive and spray salt and sand across the slope.

The bridge over the railway linked Westhaven with Arbroath Road at the east end of Carnoustie. Unlike the pedestrian wooden 'Smokey Brig' a quarter mile towards the town, it was wide enough to allow motor vehicles to cross on its wide road surface. For successive winters we, and our pals, had sledged on it – and we knew, although it wasn't a main route, that the council would ultimately spoil our fun. When snow and ice were favourable, we could slide from the top of the bridge to nearly the beach. In previous winters when the council dropped gravel on the icy surface, we (unknown to our mums and dads) ran two or three hundred yards to get a brush from the cellar at home to undo the council's work. When there was no school the next day, we were often able to sledge in gaslight until our parents came chasing us home, where we enjoyed hot chocolate beside a blazing coal fire.

* * *

When I arrived at the shop the next evening, the boss said: "Right, Robert. Forget your deliveries. I need your help at the back door. The sugar lorry's here from Cupar to deliver a ton."

The driver asked for help to carry in paper parcels, each containing fourteen bags weighing two pounds. He obviously thought I looked strong enough, because he stood on the back of the lorry and kept passing me two parcels. My heart sank and my knees buckled at the thought of carrying in a ton, and I looked at the load trying to guess what proportion was for me. Carrying fifty six pounds each trip from the lorry to the back store – where parcels were stacked on a raised wooden platform – was exhausting, but the boss helped a little. The parcels were warm, and the driver told me the sugar had been made that day. The heat was retained, and was now building up in the centre of his load. A ton of sugar meant eighty parcels of twenty-eight pounds each. I slept well that night.

Meeting Jock a few days later, I told him about my part in handling a ton of sugar.

"You insist in buying that sugar beet stuff from Cupar! We sell only the best quality cane sugar all the way from the West Indies," he scoffed.

"Ah, but are you sure barefooted people aren't trampling the canes, Jock?" I retorted jokingly, recalling his earlier jibe about Iraqi dates.

During the school Easter holiday I was occasionally asked to assemble customers' orders for delivery. This required me to move around the front shop and collect items.

"The bacon machine and meat slicer are still 'no go' areas, Robert. But you are allowed to weigh items and seal bags," the boss advised. "If you're not sure, shout for help."

All my work was checked and any mistakes were part of the learning process. However, I did have some embarrassment following an error. It all started when Cathie said we had a new weekly order. It was for Mrs Forbes' guest house in McKenzie Street, and the order was already assembled in two big wooden apple boxes.

"Jings, that'll be awkward. Could the order be put straight into the basket like the Muirdrum trip?" I asked timidly.

"No. Remember, you get a lift with the basket at Muirdrum and Travebank, but you won't get help at Mrs Forbes' place because she has no helper there. So you'll need to put both boxes into your basket."

"Should I do two runs?"

McKenzie Street was up the raised beach, and I wanted to avoid two runs.

"That's up to you, Robert," Cathie advised.

Putting both boxes into my basket, I noticed that it was going to be tricky to steer – the wooden side of the apple box ran parallel only two or three inches away from my handle-bar.

"I'll be okay, Cathie. I'll jump off and push the bike around the sharp bends."

As soon as I said that, I had a dread feeling I had made it sound easier than it would be in practice, and I believe that was when my lack of confidence began to take a grip. All went well along the High Street until I came to a slight incline approaching the junction with Station Road. Despite standing up on my pedals to get more power, the camber of the road took me on a track diagonally across the street. There was no way I could correct the curving route. Luckily no traffic was coming towards me, but I could see I was moving down the slope and heading directly for the corner doorway of Brad-burn's grocery shop.

An accident was inevitable. I felt powerless, as though time seemed to slow down. If I'd applied the brakes, the bike would have toppled. I had no choice but to keep moving. My unannounced visit into Bradburn's front shop was thankfully averted when the small front wheel of my bike hit the high kerb. The basket was catapulted onto the pavement, taking me with it, while Mrs Forbes' purchases flew towards the open front door. I scrambled – shaken but uninjured – to my feet. To experience an accident was bad enough, but to have such an almighty calamity in full view of the high street – and into the lap of a competing grocery shop – was grossly embar-rassing. My thoughts were that Bradburn's staff will forever remember the silly wee laddie from Willie Lows.

Robbie Comes a Cropper

Within seconds, two staff came rushing out to help tidy the debris. Amazingly, nothing was damaged – not even the eggs. Willie Spalding, a highly respected man in the trade who I knew was the manager, immediately asked his experienced senior apprentice Alan Ferguson to reload my boxes while I explained to Willie my bad decision to do one run.

"You've been very lucky, my boy – and your customer will never know. Why don't you do it in two runs?"

I was still shaking, but instantly felt grateful for the genuine help offered. Being accustomed to playground pranks and laughing at others' misfortunes, I was certain they would have had a giggle at my predicament. However, this was not the playground, but rather fellow grocers who understood. I was almost in tears of gratitude due to their sincere sympathy.

"Thanks, Mr Spalding. I'll come back in fifteen minutes for the second box," I said, my voice cracking.

Mrs Forbes – none the wiser – was very pleased to see me, and on my second run I got a half-crown tip. As I cycled back to the shop, I assessed the situation. I wasn't hurt except for my pride, the bike was still in one piece, the order had survived, and Cathie and the boss would never know – unless Willie told them, and I had a feeling that he wouldn't. There was some guilt, but no lasting damage was done and I was given a handsome tip. A lucky lesson.

* * *

It was a cold and blustery Saturday forenoon when I had to make one of my usual deliveries to Westhaven. As I crossed the railway line and turned into Tayside Street, I came across a scene which brought back memories. It was Peem and Billy struggling with a massive one hundred weight bag of cinders. I knew exactly what they were doing, because I used to do that same chore.

Billy's parents had learned a few years previously that the gasworks in Bonella Street sold bags of coke – not ashes but cinders, produced when the coal was burned in the gas works. A hundred weight was much bulkier than the same weight of coal, and Billy used his trailer or 'bogie' to transport a bag for each family. It required two trips. I recalled the problem; the bag was so ungainly that it kept slipping off Billy's cart. Saturday collections from the gasworks took up an entire morning, as the journeys were constantly interrupted by the bag falling off.

"Gee, we're glad to see you Robbie!" said Billy as he wiped his already-blackened face with an even blacker hand.

I had a few minutes to spare, and I could see they were exhausted as they wrestled with the almost immovable object. So I put my bike on its stand and went to help.

"Right: one, two, three... lift!" I cried, and as the bogie kept moving away we managed to get the giant bag onboard.

"Thanks, Robbie!" they gasped. "Can you stay with us?"

"Sorry, but I've got to deliver this and then get back to the shop. There are orders piling up for me."

I didn't enjoy leaving them, and went on my way only to find upon my return that they had barely moved a hundred yards – with another four hundred to go – and the bag was again off the bogie. So I stopped to help.

"Can ye gie us a hand?" asked Billy, his face now even blacker and smudged with sweat.

"You'll need to hurry. I have a full day of deliveries ahead."

"Can we no' put some coke in yer basket?" asked Peem.

"Tell you what; fill up my two boxes in the basket and that will help."

Billy and Peem started to fill the boxes with their bare hands, and soon we loaded them onto the bike. We then moved the bag back on the bogie, and I left them to wheel it while I cycled to Billy's house and waited for them to catch up. We lifted the boxes out of my basket, and they were at last home.

"That's oor first run. Now we need to go the 'Gassie' for the next. Can ye no' come back and help?" Peem asked.

"You're joking!" I laughed. "I've lost my boxes, and now I'm late. The boss will kill me."

As I cycled away, I felt cruel because I knew – from having done the same chore the previous winter – that they had a huge task on their hands.

* * *

In addition to my recent accident at Bradburn's, I had another big learning step when I answered the shop telephone for the first time. This happened quite by chance. Staff were serving, and I was alone in the back shop when the phone rang in the makeshift desk area. It was never clear to me why the phone was not in the boss's office. As the boss rushed past me, he said: "My hands are greasy. Just see who it is, Robert. Go, go, greasy grocer go!"

We didn't have a telephone at home – only a few people I knew did – but while in the Cub Scouts I'd had a training session on how to use one. Baguera took three of us, just a few minutes away from the hut, to the iconic British red telephone box with many small panes of glass. There were identical boxes at various key places all over the town, and I had stepped inside a few and always found them with litter on the floor and a horrible stink of cigarette smoke. I knew only that if I put money in the slot, dialled the number and then someone answered, I had to press button 'A'. On hearing the coins drop down inside the money box, I would be able to talk until the pips sounded to tell me that my time was up. If, having put my money in, no one answered the dialling tone then I would press button 'B' and get my money back. Knowing how buttons 'A' and 'B' worked was helpful, but I'd never had a phone conversation in my life. Nervously, I picked up the heavy black receiver and tried to untwist the cord.

"Hello?" I said.

"Good evening. Is that Wm Low and Company?" a posh, cultured voice enquired.

"Yes."

"Who's speaking?"

"Robert."

"Oh, good. Will you ask Cathie to add a few things to my order for tomorrow, please?"

"Yes."

For too long I kept the lady waiting while I looked for a notepad and pencil. Panicking, I tore a scrap off a nearby paper bag and luckily found a pencil.

"Sorry," I stammered.

"A can of peaches – that's the two and sixpence size – a quarter of 'Willow' gold label tea, and half a pound of bourbon cream biscuits, please."

As I was noting the details, I caught a glimpse of Mr Munro – the area manager – walking past me on his way to the back store, probably to make his routine inspection. Being so shocked, I spoke into the phone "thank you," and then replaced the receiver.

When Cathie came back from counter duty, I gave her my scribbled note and told her about a lady who wanted to add things to her order. "Who was it, Robert?"

"It was... oh!"

I was speechless. Mr Munro's unexpected presence had distracted me, and I'd forgotten to ask. But by a process of elimination and the clues of 'gold label tea' and the cultured voice, Cathie worked out it that it had been Mrs Stewart.

"Gosh!" I gasped. "Was that the director's wife? I should have recognised her voice."

That was the bad news! With my worst fears ringing in my head, I delivered her groceries the next day.

"You did well, Robert. But ask Mr Stewart to tell you how to take an order over the phone," said Mrs Stewart, who was extremely pleasant.

What a relief! But guessing she would check with the boss, I had to ask him. He gave me instructions on how to answer, and told me where to find a notepad and pencil. That was one way of learning how to deal with a customer. It was after that I began to wear a pencil behind my right ear. Luckily Mr Munro had been completely unaware of my mistake.

All he said to me was: "How are you getting on, Robert?"

"Fine thanks, Mr Munro."

This was the first time he'd spoken to me, and I found him to be pleasant – which was at odds with comments made by the staff, who said how tough he was. In fact, they referred to him as 'Munro'. He had a habit of parking his black Triumph Mayflower car in the centre of town, and I had been told to keep an eye open for it when out and about and get back to the shop to warn the boss. Mr Munro was always exceptionally well-dressed in a dark suit, white shirt and colourful tie. When it was cold he wore a heavy tweed coat and a trilby hat. He was tall and well-built, with a bronzed complexion and black hair that was going silver at the sides. I hadn't seen the film *The Barefoot Contessa*, but more than once I overheard the shop staff refer to him as Rossano Brazzi; they said he reminded them of the heart throb Italian actor who had the lead role.

His customary procedure, while sternly studying the window displays, was to tuck his black attaché case under his left arm. Was he giving the boss marks out of ten, I wondered? He always went on a shop walkabout before speaking to the boss, and didn't talk to me. He'd probably forgiven –

but not forgotten – a time when, some months earlier, I had come rushing into the back shop, having cycled along the High Street at great speed to loudly report that "Munro's on his way! His car's at Park Avenue!"... only to meet him eye to eye coming out of the boss's office. We stared at each other, but nothing was said. It was one of those moments when time seemed to stand still. I regarded Mr Munro as a true professional businessman, and didn't mean any disrespect. I thought I was being helpful.

* * *

I was counting my tips on Saturday evening when mum came into my bedroom. "I hope you're remembering that we've got a big day tomorrow, Robert!" she said excitedly.

Her enthusiasm initially confused me, and then I remembered. "Oh yes! The christening tomorrow."

"Yes, and we've all got to be up early. Then dad has to meet auntie Jean off the bus from Montrose. I've got your shirt and trousers ironed, but you'll need to brush your shoes."

Auntie Jean was mum's twin sister, and I didn't understand why she had to come to church with us.

"Why is auntie Jean coming here?"

"She's Jean's godmother, and she's going to carry Jean into the church."

It was then I realised a lot of thinking and planning had gone into the big day, and even began to realise where Jean's name came from.

"Now, we need to be at the church at 10.45 all bright and tidy, so you and James need to have a bath tonight. I've got the boiler fire on already."

On my way in, I'd seen all the bikes were outside the wash house. But I hadn't thought why, and didn't connect it with Jean's christening. But of course, mum would have planned that Peem and I would have to have to be scrubbed and clean for the big event. Luckily it was a dry day, but cold, and we must have been quite a procession walking from Admiral Street across the Steenie Brig to the church. Peem, Isobel and myself sat in the front pew as usual, along with other Sunday school pupils.

Mum, dad and auntie Jean were near the baptismal font in what was usually a choir pew. I can remember thinking it was beginning to be quite a different day for us. I'd seen christenings previously, but now it was my family's day. As I sat there watching the proceedings, I had the feeling of a family history event. In all my life I must have been at Peem and Isobel's christenings, but now this was unique because I was old enough to witness my wee sister's baptism.

My mind went back to the day I sat in the playground worrying about mum. Was she sick? Would she die? And my embarrassment at the shock of learning that my mum was expecting a baby. How I had been unwilling to accept reality, and that day at my Scout camp when I knew mum was 'different' and needed help. Skipper's observation was the first piece of evidence outside of my own world that mum was indeed going to have a baby. It was Skipper, too, who gave me the comforting congratulations on the evening baby Jean was born. Now, watching all this, I had become quite a proud big brother.

* * *

When long, sunny June evenings came around, Peem and I planned a surprise for our granny and grandad at Woodside Croft near Dunninald, just a few miles south of Montrose. We were to cycle the nineteen miles from Westhaven, and return the same Saturday evening. Bikes had long since been a large part of our lives that we thought we could do it without the need for lights. Dad had always guided us on maintenance: oiling wheels and chains, how to keep tyres hard and fix a puncture, how to adjust the seat height as we grew taller, and generally what we needed to do in order to keep our bikes in good condition. I had three gears on my bike and – with panniers fitted – had cycled to the Roundhouse youth hostel at Glenisla with Scout pals for an overnight stay, so I was quite confident. Peem was less experienced and had no gears, but he was fitter and stronger than me.

"Now, you must look after each other. Don't be separated, watch out for traffic, and use your hand signals," mum stressed as she stood watching us prepare.

"I dinna hae gears, so Robert will have to wait for me on the hilly parts," Peem said, realising I may find it easier.

"Yes, Robert – don't rush ahead up Arbekie Brae at Inverkeiler. Stay beside James," dad added as he checked Peem's tyres.

"What are you taking with you?" mum enquired.

"We've got lemonade in my panniers, and I have our waterproofs and a repair kit in there too."

"That's fine, but here's some cakes and biscuits for you when you stop for a break."

"Thanks, mum! We'll take that," I said as I packed the bags in my side carriers.

This was quite an undertaking, as I had been on my message bike until nearly 5 o'clock, but we had waited for our chosen warm and dry evening with no wind.

I had asked the boss if I could get away early if all my orders were complete, and we were able to set off at 5.30. I had travelled to Woodside on the bus with the family many times, but once out on the road the journey took on a different perspective and the only guides I had were landmarks I'd seen from the bus.

Although acquainted with the route, and well on the way to Arbroath, I became nervously aware of the enormity of our journey. I had never been on such an expedition to Woodside without mum and dad, and I had a strange mixture of fear, excitement and bravado with my senses tuned to everything around me. Road traffic was minimal; we saw just the occasional car, and no other cyclists. It was then I realised that that while this was an epic trek for us, any bystander would simply have accepted we were two boys on bikes out for a run.

We passed the cottage in the woods beyond Arbroath, and saw the tree dad said he'd fallen from when he was a boy. He'd broken his nose, and was unconscious for an hour.

Our first stop for a rest and a bite was at Inverkeiler village, and it was here that I had more than a glimpse of where dad had spent his school days. He had told me he walked two miles from Lunan to school, and I sat there trying to picture dad as a boy running around the playground. I'd seen his school prize books, and now I had the sense of a part of his life. I'd only seen sepia photographs of him as a young person, and he always looked lean, tidy and serious. I knew him as an adult – gentle, courteous and quiet natured. He never smoked or drank alcohol, and I never heard him swear.

On occasions when he hurt himself – say a finger, while re-pairing something – his favourite expression was 'oh, you bonny laddie'.

Arbekie Brae did prove for Peem to be his greatest challenge, and I kept going for I found the stop-start routine more tiring. I had time to sit at the top of the hill and gaze down on Lunan Bay while Peem caught up and took his well-earned rest.

"You were meant to stay beside me," he complained.

"It's alright. No traffic about, and you were in my sights all the time."

Lunan was where grandad had been station master, and where dad was born – one of four children – on 6th De-cember 1914. Being out in the fresh air and getting the scents of the salty sea and the blossoms of the countryside gave me an even closer link with dad, which in all my bus journeys I'd never had. Where he had worked, gone to church, acted in village plays, and the routes he must have taken when he told us tales of walking to and from Montrose cinemas and dances. The hard work was over, and we seemed to glide on to the White Inn where we had quenching gulps of lemonade. At this point I had another close connection never previously experienced: it was to look down the road towards granny's croft and then, in the distance, to see amongst the trees parts of Dunninald Castle where mum as a young woman had worked before marrying dad. She had told us tales of her du-ties as a maid, and how she had learned how to cook and bake. The black and white pictures I had seen of mum as a lean, fit young person when she worked at the castle didn't show the reddish hair which she had. For some reason she was quite nervous and highly strung, and became quite emo-tional when relating sad tales – even though they didn't directly affect her. She was tireless in her efforts to look after all of us, even when we grew up and left home.

Mum, a twin, was born three days before dad, and was one of eight children – the oldest of whom left school at fourteen and went on to become Chief CID Inspector of Aberdeen City Police. Again, this close feel and connection to mum and dad's world was strong. Here we were in the land of our parents: the setting for all the stories of what they had done, where they worked and played, and now I could relate to them better. Without pedalling, we rushed down the hill to the croft.

"I'll be there first!" Peem shouted to me over his shoulder.

"Stop at the crossroads," I called back.

Peem ignored the stop at the quiet country road and was first to the croft gate. As we walked into the yard, grandad was coming in from his fields carrying two rabbits he'd caught in snares.

"Well, well! It's the Carnoustie boys," he said in his usual strong farmer's voice as he laid down the fresh-looking animals.

"Come away in," he said as he led the way into the low-ceilinged cottage. "Look who's here, mum! Two bikers all the way from Carnoustie."

"Goodness me! You haven't cycled all that way, have you?" she asked as she stopped making butter in her hand-held churn. "What's wrong?"

"Nothing, granny. We just came to say hello."

"I'll make you a cup of tea. Would one of you finish this off?" she asked as she held out the churn, which Peem knowingly and quickly grasped and started turning the blades. The churn was a large bottle (not unlike a large sweetie jar on display in shops) with blades inside which turned the cream. The blades were rotated by turning a handle at the top of the churn. Peem had previously made butter, and knew that after some time the task of turning became more difficult as the butter began to form. But he could see the cream wasn't yet at that stage.

While Peem churned, I sat in a chair beside granny's large square table and pictured us and our cousins seated around it enjoying the tastiest of meals when we holidayed there to help grandad on the farm. We probably took granny's meals for granted then, but looking back her rabbit stews, hare soups, pheasant pies, and strawberries and fresh cream were luxuries.

The bright sun of a June evening shone through the small window into the tidy room, with a large brass paraffin lamp hanging from one of the bacon hooks in the ceiling almost above the large, blackened fire grate. The rays, like a spotlight, lit up my grandad's Scottish Horticultural Society ornate certificate which recognised his 40 ¼ years of service as grieve at nearby Boddin Farm. I always marvelled at that, as I could never conceive how he also farmed the three fields of his croft.

I knew this room well. Peem and I had lived with granny when we came for 'tattie howkin' on grandad's fields. Everything about it was quaint and comfortable.

While we enjoyed a welcome cup of tea and one of her special Frost's (the local Montrose baker) perkin biscuits, Granny asked us how we were and how everybody was at home. We chatted for a while, and then it was seven thirty and time to go.

"Can I have a look around the yard, granny, before we go?" I asked.

"Aye, of course. You won't see much change, though."

I looked at all the places I knew so well; the hen houses and runs where I collected eggs, the sties where I'd helped feed the pigs, the straw stack where cousin Sandy had taught me how to catch birds under a sieve, and the byre where Maisie – granny's milk cow – was housed.

"Haste ye back!" granny and grandad called out in their accustomed way as we set off, and I couldn't help thinking we'd left behind a Scottish farming time capsule with a sample of how life may have been a hundred years or more before. Granny and grandad gave me a sense of two contented, hard-working people living in a unique world. A world so unlike my own.

With no nasty hills for Peem to cope with and hardly any cars about, we were able to cycle alongside each other most of the way home, giving us time to reminisce about our previous visits to Woodside.

"I remember seeing granny one Easter, years ago, standing in her garden with a big wicker basket full of coloured eggs ready to be handed out," said Peem as he free-wheeled along.

"We had some great times there when we met our cousins. Do you remember the Christmas tree with real candles burning, and little gifts tied on for each of us?"

"I do! And you trying to sing 'Westering Home' as your party piece!"

"Watch it, Peem, or I'll leave you behind on the big hill at Inverkeiler."

We travelled home in good time with no incidents, and recalled our many happy days when so many of our aunties, uncles and cousins assembled on Sundays at the Woodside family hub. It was, for me, not only a real treat to make an unexpected trip to Woodside, but a chance to share adventure and fun with Peem.

Arriving home safely on a perfect early summer evening, we gave mum and dad a detailed report during which Peem made an expected request.

"I want to do bike runs like Robert did with his Scout pals, but I need gears."

"Mum and I have been speaking about this, and we've decided we're going to get you a new bicycle," dad said.

"Jings! A new bike for Peem. He's the first in the family to get that!" The run to granny and grandad's croft had produced a surprise for Peem. He was ecstatic.

After a supper bite, I strolled to the ballaster and saw the tide was out and that the sea was almost a flat calm. I took stock of our cycle trip, and couldn't believe what I had learned during the evening visit to the croft. It wasn't really all that far away; within my physical reach without a bus. I had sensed mum and dad's world, and now I could connect my world of Westhaven with theirs and my busy life as a message boy was part of my growing up. That one trip gave me a strong link with my heritage, and taught me something else – that travelling like that gives a greater connection with the world around us.

It was Monday morning before I knew it, and I was cycling furiously back to the shop from the Anderson Grice delivery just as the school bell was ringing. I was well and truly back in my world.

CHAPTER 10

My Anniversary, or "I Brought You Into the World!"

July 1954

"CAN you try and help James with his homework tonight, Robert?" mum asked me as soon as I arrived home. "He's not sure where to start," She added as she laid a plate of cold ham salad down on the table in front of me.

The end of the school year approached, and our teachers kept us busy almost to the last day so it was no surprise that Peem had some homework. I had been asked to précis newspaper reports of recent events, and also had some work to do.

"What have you to write about?" I enquired.

"We were given choices and told to write about 300 words," he said. "I could write about them all, but I don't know which one to choose."

"What choices did you get?"

"What is my favourite form of transport and why?"

"Well, which one do you think would be best?"

"I don't know. I could write about buses or even cycling, but that seems too boring."

"We're only a hundred yards from the railway line and you've seen lots of engines pass by the end of Admiral Street, and you've been to London on a train. Would you like me to jot down ideas to get you started? Then you could try to write something and let me see it," I suggested.

"Alright," Peem replied with a bit more cheer.

The next evening, he handed me his first attempt, written in pencil:

I have been to Greenock by train for a summer holiday, and to London on a train pulled by the *Flying Scotsman* which I think is the best engine I have ever seen. I live close to the railway which links Aberdeen to London. My friends and I often sit beside the railway line and write notes about the names of the steam engines we see. I always like to imagine the trains we see coming to a halt at Kings Cross, London, and often wish I could travel on them. My dad has told me the trains which go past at great speed are the long- distance ones, and those which stop at Carnoustie station are slower local trains. The 'fasts' are pulled by engines designed by Sir Arthur Peppercorn, with names like *Aberdonian* and *Blue Peter*, and others such as *Flying Scotsman* and *Sir Nigel Gresley*, both designed by Sir Nigel Gresley. Sometimes we see engines with no names, only numbers, and the one we see most is 60009.

Although I wish I could travel every day on a 'fast', I like the local trains because the drivers and firemen on board always wave back to us. Sometimes my dad tells us when the Royal Train is going to pass by, and my friends and I like to make sure we are there to wave to the driver and hope to see the Queen looking out from her window at us in Westhaven. The Royal train is always quieter and slower than all other trains, and seems to glide along. When I grow up I would like to be an engine driver and travel to and from London every day.

I like travelling by train best because it is more comfortable than buses and bicycles as I can walk about. The compartments are warm, and there are usually framed paintings of various holiday places in Britain.

"That's very good, Peem. But I think you could add something about the countryside you see from the train, and add something about the smell of coal and steam which comes from the engine."

Peem added some pieces and happily re-wrote his composition using his pen-nib and ink.

"I got eight marks out of ten," he reported later. "Now I realise we see another world passing by the end of our street every day," he said as he proudly showed me his teacher's approving red ticks on the page.

* * *

One day the boss asked me to help clear a large space on the back shop floor.

"We're getting a fridge next Monday," he said, grinning from ear to ear while moving boxes out of the planned area.

"Gee, it must be a big one," I responded excitedly.

"You're right. I'll be six feet square with standing room inside," he smiled, indicating the area with outstretched arms.

"What will we be storing in it?" I asked.

"All our bacon, cans of cooked meats, and soft butter and lard in summer months," the boss happily listed.

"That should mean it'll be easier to handle stock."

"It's better than that, because it will be less... what?" he posed the question.

"Waste?" I hastily replied.

"Right first time: you're learning. Only Munro's best branches are getting a fridge. Our record sales have helped to buy it," he proudly stated.

I could see the boss's obvious pleasure at being told he was in the top bracket of branches. And I felt good too, for I could sense the branch was being successful. Looking back, it was an important milestone in provisions handling in the grocery trade: better handling, less waste, and cleaner, safer products for consumers. A week later I arrived from school to find the fridge in place and working. It was fitted with hooks on rails and wooden, slatted shelves. With summer coming this would transform the whole procedure of how we stored our bacon, cooked meats and butter. It had an internal light, and I stepped inside to examine it. Just then someone closed the door, and I was plunged into darkness. I panicked. I'd no idea what had happened, and immediately had a vision of being locked up all night and dying a slow death. What seemed like minutes later, the door was opened by Dot.

"That's dangerous, Dot! I could've been locked in there all night!"

"No, look at this. The fridge can be opened or closed from the outside, but this is a release lever in case you get trapped inside," she said, pointing to a metal rod on the inside of the door. It was her way of making sure I knew a way out. On that first Monday evening while I was putting bacon into the fridge, the boss happily advised: "No need to check for maggots now, Robert."

"That's good news!"

"But remember; don't leave the door open too long, because it'll warm up and use more electricity. Go, go, greasy grocer go!"

It was more progress, and just another example of the boss being careful with his pennies. I'd seen an improvement in dealing with sugar, and now our provisions handling was revolutionised, bringing more efficiency to the business.

It seemed to be a time when the company implemented change, as another new development related to the on-going battle with mice. Evidently the man who came to check shop hygiene had recommended to the company that the old way of catching vermin had to be replaced with a new method. Mr Stewart told me he'd never used the new method, but he showed me how the system worked. First, he told me to cut a piece of cardboard about twelve inches square, and then spread what he called treacle on it. He explained the substance was really a resin. I asked him if it was that simple, and he added that I had to put poisoned food pellets in a tray alongside the cardboard to attract the mice. We had an almost immediate result: four dead mice glued on the resin on my first check!

Setting up the procedure took time and was potentially messy compared to traps, but the system caught more mice and I didn't have to touch them! I simply rolled up the cardboard and carefully disposed of it. The white pellets seemed to have the added effect of shrinking and drying the dead mice, which was also more hygienic.

One evening, on arriving from school, I checked to find three dead mice but a fourth still moving its tail. It must have recently been trapped when out for an afternoon stroll for a biscuit crumb. Not wishing to see it in this distressed state, I took the sticky trap outside and – with the aid of an empty Parazone bottle – finished off the poor creature. How many mice had escaped death when there had been only one trap?

The mouse trapping worked very well, and the pest control officer (the ladies on the staff called him the 'mousey man') who had introduced the system eventually reported to the boss that we had eradicated the problem. Consequently, I was told I didn't have to set up the trap every evening; just once a week as a check. Another welcome time-saving improvement.

Message boy life continued happily, and I couldn't believe it when my first anniversary came along. As I lay in bed that night, I tried to mentally list all the things I'd learned in a year. How to speak to customers and cope with the ever-changing weather, and to recognise black ice. Learning some shop practices such as stock rotation, facing up shelves, and assembling orders. Dealing with giant deliveries to the country areas, and discovering the most efficient way to pack boxes into the basket. Strangely, the scariest and most worrying things had turned out to be easier than I imagined, like getting a new battery from the boss. Then the experience of dealing with a spider in the banana box. The people I'd met, such as friendly Freddie the boxer and the frighteningly efficient Miss Black. All of my experiences I could cope with again, except one: taking a girl to a dance.

There had been a lot of experiences and learning from mistakes, and I made a mental note to ask Jock if he had made a list of his progress.

As I cycled along the High Street one day, I met by chance Johnny the butcher's boy as he slouched along the pavement displaying his usual couldn't-care-less attitude.

"Where's your message bike?" I enquired while braking to speak with him.

"Dinna ken, dinna care. Left the job," he mumbled as he kicked an imaginary object along the pavement.

"What was wrong?"

"Ach, it was awfi borin'. Nothing but potted hough, and hardly any tips."

My reaction was that Johnny had probably started his job full of hope, just as I had done, but unfortunately things had not progressed beyond doing small deliveries whereas my boss had taken the trouble to make use of me in jobs all around the shop. I had variety in my work, and I had new challenges almost every week. In contrast, my job had turned out exactly as the boss had said – "More than delivering boxes" – which was my good fortune. The Co-op surely didn't see the need to develop an apprentice butcher. The basic job may have suited Jim, but it was my huge luck that he introduced me to Freddie. When I thought about it later that night, I had another idea. Perhaps Jim knew it was a limited job and didn't want me to be bored like poor Johnny.

"Is there no chance of another job somewhere Johnny?" I asked, attempting to cheer him up.

"Ach, it's nae use. The jobs are a' taken noo," he said as he slouched on his way.

As I pedalled off, I tried to think of any prospects for him. But I had to admit he was probably right, although I harboured the thought that Johnny was possibly the kind of lad who didn't see chances of how to grow in his old job.

* * *

One evening I knocked on a new customer's door in a block of flats. A very friendly, plump lady with bright eyes and rosy cheeks answered.

"Messages from Lows, Mrs Ramsay."

"Oh, thank you, son." When she came back with the empty box she asked: "Are you Robert?"

"Yes."

"And what's your second name?"

When I told her, she said she knew mum.

"Oh!" I responded with surprise.

"Yes, I'm Nurse Ramsay, and it was me who brought you into the world. How's your mum?"

Her amazing announcement had me spellbound, and I can't remember how I replied but she added: "Tell her I'm asking for her."

With that exciting news, I rushed home and told mum that evening.

"Oh yes, that's true. Nurse Ramsay was my nurse. She was always very kind and cheery. I haven't seen her for many years. How is she?"

"Fine. She's friendly, and gave me a shilling."

"Next time, tell her I'm asking for her and say you have an eleven year old brother and a nine year old sister. And remember to tell her about baby Jean."

How many people ever meet the nurse who delivered them? I couldn't stop thinking that Nurse Ramsay and I were in the delivery business. Must tell Jock that I'd met a lady who had delivered a very high quality product.

Thereafter I addressed her as Nurse Ramsay. Each time I delivered her groceries, I wanted to ask questions about my arrival in the world. Was I a normal birth? Did she hang me upside down and spank me to start me breathing like I'd seen in films? But I never plucked up the courage.

A few weeks later, Cathie told me I had another new customer: a Mrs Smith.

"You'll probably know her daughter; she was Akaela the Cub Mistress."

"Oh no!" I said without thinking.

"Why, what's wrong with you?"

I told Cathie I had done a very silly thing about four years previously during my Cub camp at Tannadice, near Finavon. And that, after all that time, Miss Smith still made fun of me every time we met. Even in the street, she shouted: "Robert Murray, clean that dixie!".

"Well, I'm sure she didn't mean it badly. But what is a dixie, anyway?" Cathie asked.

"It's a large, oval-shaped deep cooking pot, big enough to serve a camp of Cubs with a bowl of soup. Miss Smith asked me to clean out all the dixies, which I started to do, and when I came to one with bones and water in it I tipped the lot into the kitchen sump. Later she asked me where the stock for soup was, and I told her I didn't know. She let out a scream and jumped around in the kitchen. Other cub mistresses gathered round as well as some other Cubs, and she told them what had happened. I felt a real idiot, but secretly I thought I had done what I was asked to do."

"Tell me more later," Cathie interrupted. "I'm busy right now."

I cycled to her address praying Miss Smith wouldn't answer the door, but my desperate wish was not answered.

"Messages from Lows," I said when she opened the door.

"Oh, thank you, Robert."

When she returned with the empty box she gave me a shilling tip. I was amazed to find that Miss Smith was normal to me for the first time since my camp nearly four years earli-er.

Cathie was busy when I returned, but later when we were cleaning up at closing time she asked me if I still wanted to tell my story. I told her the tale, but deep down I didn't want to do so because I thought it would make me seem so stupid.

"Well, I made that terrible mistake one day in the camp kitchen, which was an outdoor area marked off with string and with plate racks made of wooden sticks and a mug tree.

"Did she give you a dressing down?"

"No, she didn't give me a telling off, and I didn't lose any badges. But I know I should have asked for help."

"That was an easy mistake to make, and you did what you were asked. I think she realised she hadn't given a clear instruction," Cathie said.

"I've never told my mum and dad about my mistake. You're the first person I've ever told."

"I wouldn't worry about it. Maybe Miss Smith realises her mistake and just wants to make a joke about it."

After Cathie told me that I felt a lot better and the next time I delivered Akaela's groceries I plucked up courage to speak.

"I'm sorry I made that big mistake at the Cub camp."

"You're not still worried about that, are you?"

"I've never forgotten it."

"Well, it was all my fault!"

She smiled and gave me a shilling, and I was so relieved after four years of torment that I seemed to float along on my bike back to the shop like I'd never done before.

* * *

During summer, the army camp at Barry Buddon was busy with Territorial Army (TA) soldiers billeted there for training. It was not unusual for senior ranks to visit the shop, without warning, and buy huge quantities of produce: bread, butter, eggs, bacon, cooked meats, cans of beans. They often wiped out entire stocks of some products. Additionally, Miss Jennings – who ran the Soldier's Home café at Buddon – would telephone and look for immediate delivery of similar products. It was a long bike ride out of town past Barry village until I found a short cut, via a rough lane which ran past the laundry and emerged near the railway station. When I reached the camp gates, my duty was to report at the sentry box. Like the Jammy, it was a commercial delivery and no tip.

A four-week period during July and August went flying past when the Taylor family arrived by train, as usual, for their two week annual holiday. Charles couldn't wait to get on the rocks and fish, but had to delay until I was available as my full-time work kept me busy. As planned, the Christies then arrived for the first time, and I remember thinking they wouldn't like it so much because the children were younger. But it was a glorious summer with swimming, paddling, and games at the ballaster in the evenings. When the time came to depart they were Carnoustie converts, and booked the same two weeks for 1955. In those days, the Town Council made huge efforts to attract holiday makers. Every month from June to September, a programme was posted on boards all over the town, advertising everything from the monthly Carnoustie Princess competitions to games with Uncle George: sand building, putting, treasure-hunting, and the popular 'Go as You Please' talent shows every Thursday evening.

The town looked welcoming and tidy, with flower baskets hanging on every lamp post in the High Street. The popularity of the town was evident when, on Friday afternoons, taxis were lined up the length of Station Road awaiting another train-load of families from the central belt of Scotland to be despatched to their holiday lodgings.

Mum, in common with many house-holders in the town, benefitted financially from the growing popularity of the town and the breezy, bracing coastline of Angus – long before the lure to Lanzarote and other exotic holiday spots.

* * *

The only hitch I had with the boss cropped up one day in July. "Robert, we're running out of lettuce and I haven't had time to order them. So off you go to Mr McKenzie and get four dozen. Tell him that you need them in a hurry. Do you know where his market garden is?"

"Yes, in Wallace Street."

"Good. Take some empty Dutch tomato boxes with you. Go, go, greasy grocer go."

Quickly pedalling off, I reached the garden cottage within minutes. I rang the doorbell and knocked loudly to no effect. As I walked about the gardens looking for Mr McKenzie, I called out his name. No luck. Finally, I found him on his hands and knees in a greenhouse.

"Mr McKenzie? Can I have four dozen lettuce for Lows, please?"

"What?" He seemed deaf, so I had to repeat loudly.

Mr McKenzie looked ancient and took ages to stand up. I could see he had been a very tall, well-built man, but now his whole body looked stiff as he shuffled slowly in a stooped fashion and I could only admire his ability to keep running his immaculate market garden at his age. We moved at a snail's pace to the other end of his nursery, where I saw where the lettuce grew. It was an agonisingly slow journey. He produced a penknife from his waistcoat pocket and, grasping a lettuce in one hand, cut it while leaving the root in the ground. Then, one by one, he took each lettuce to a water tap where he washed them and packed each one upside down in my tomato boxes. It was an excruciatingly long-winded process. The boss wanted them quickly, but I could see no way of speeding up Mr McKenzie because he was so precise in everything he did. Eventually, with every precious lettuce packed, I pedalled as fast as possible back to the shop.

The boss looked unusually cross and said: "Where on earth have you been, Robert? Have you been gossiping with your pals?"

"No, I had to wait for Mr McKenzie." The boss had probably never seen the gardener's slow motion, and I sensed it was a weak answer. It seemed pointless to argue, but I was hurt the boss thought I had been wasting time.

"Well, you'll have to go out and deliver now."

So there I was, back on the bike to the same end of the town delivering lettuce.

Those varied experiences were valuable. As time passed, my confidence grew and I plucked up the courage to bank my tips with Miss Black. But this time I handed over my bank book and cloth bag with coins already sorted and counted; no syrup can, and no buttons! I couldn't wait to tell mum my banking procedure with Miss Black was without incident, and as I cycled home I saw the funny side of it and tried to invent an appropriate film title. The best one I could manage was *Scared to Save*.

CHAPTER 11

Another Big Step, or "A Brown One, Mrs Nimble?"

October 1954

WHEN I arrived home from school one Tuesday evening I found my nine year old sister, Isobel, curled up in dad's rocking chair and in tears.

"What's wrong with Isobel?" I asked mum as I hung up my jacket on a peg in the hall.

"She was told off by her teacher, Miss Murray, for talking in class," mum said while setting the table.

"Oh yes, I remember she was strict."

"But Isobel says she wasn't the one who was speaking, and now she has to write fifty lines repeating 'I must not speak in class'."

When I think back, Miss Murray was a Mary Poppins lookalike with no bike, but quite severe – although my mum told me she was a most sincere person.

It was, to my knowledge, the first time Isobel had been in trouble, and I wondered what I could do to help calm her because I remembered quite vividly how I felt when Miss Murray upset me.

"Come with me and see how my tadpoles are coming on in the big jar on my bedroom window sill," I suggested. "Will you promise to save up any raw white of eggs when mum is baking and drop some into the jar? Tadpoles seem to like that."

"Yes, I'll do that."

Once we were inside the room I shared with Peem, I tried to turn her mind away from Miss Murray. Isobel was a sensitive girl, always eager to do things well – especially her dancing. She was slim and dainty on her toes, and was forever cheery with a giggly laugh.

"Look – nearly all my tadpoles have got four legs now, and their tails are slowly disappearing. Soon they'll be climbing out, and mum will be telling me they'll have to go."

"Where will you put them?"

"I always take them to the wee burn beside Newton Panbride church and set them free."

"Will they be safe there?"

"Of course. They'll be very happy. That's where they should be."

"I'm glad to hear that. I've always worried about them."

"Listen, Isobel," I said, changing the subject. "I've never told mum this, but Miss Murray once gave me a hundred lines to write for speaking in class, and I thought she didn't like me. But two or three days after I wrote them, she asked me to be the paper monitor for a day, then two days later to hand out raffia to everybody in the class."

"I'm very glad to hear that. But what's a paper monitor?" she asked, turning away from my tadpole jar.

"Well, she didn't have jotters for us because I think there were still wartime shortages. So I had to go around the class and hand out sheets of toilet paper."

"Toilet paper?"

"Yes, that was all we had to do our arithmetic work on."

"Really? That was awful."

"Well, yes, it was hopeless. But it wasn't that bad, because in those days we did most of our work on a slate board."

"What's a slate board?"

"It was a piece of slate – like you'd get off a roof – with a wooden frame around it, and which fitted into my school bag."

"What did you write with?"

"We had to use a thin stick of hard chalk."

"That must have been difficult."

"It was a great nuisance. I accidentally kept breaking my chalk stick inside my school bag. Not only that; we had to take to school every day a tiny bottle of water and a dry cloth so we could wipe our board clear after we had our work checked."

"And what is raffia?"

"Oh, that was long strands of stuff like flat plastic string which came in different colours. We used it for craft work."

"We don't do anything like that now."

Isobel listened to my ideas about looking after tadpoles and to my story of how Miss Murray had become quite normal. She wiped away her tears and began to relax, and didn't mention her fifty lines at all during tea, after which she settled down happily to write her punishment. When I heard her ask mum if she could practise her Sailor's Hornpipe and Irish Washerwoman's Dances, I knew she had overcome her shock.

"You'll never guess, Robert; Miss Murray asked me to be the ink monitor today," Isobel reported two days later.

"Gee, filling up everybody's ink wells! That was more difficult than handing out toilet paper," I encouraged.

* * *

About a week later, Peem – who was last home from school – burst almost breathlessly into the living room.

"Has it arrived yet?" he asked.

"Yes, and we're all here waiting for you to see it working," said mum as she stirred a mixture in her baking bowl.

"What are you making?" Peem asked.

"I thought it would be a good idea to bake some pancakes on the brand new hotplate," mum said as she switched on the sparkling black and cream new arrival: an electric cooker.

It was a modern appliance, complete with two hotplates, a coiled cooking element for pots on the hob, and an oven fitted below. Mum hadn't had many new things in her life, but this was now her pride and joy.

She placed a spoonful of cake mix on the greased hot surface and we all gathered round to see the pancakes cook. In a matter of minutes, we could smell the mouth-watering aroma of hot pancakes and mum deftly turned each one over.

"Can I make some?" asked Peem.

"Yes, but let's put some jam and butter on this batch and taste them first."

We each sampled the delicacy from our new cooker and finished off a plate of pancakes seemingly in an instant. Peem was coached on what heat to use, how to prepare the mix, how much to put on the hotplate, and how to flip over each pancake.

"Now you can make pancakes whenever you like, but you must be careful and follow the rules – and you can only do it when Robert is with you," mum advised. My first domestic responsibility: pancake supervisor.

Isobel and I had our turn, and we then washed and tidied each implement. It was a huge novelty, and for the next week or so we devoured several platefuls of our newly-acquired product.

Mum was delighted with her new cooker, which served her well, and she continued to produce all my favourites: melting moments, cakes, birthday dumplings (complete with silver threepenny pieces wrapped in wax paper), Irish stews, and my greatest treat of all – her rice pudding, containing raisins and topped off with a rippling, roasted top skin straight out of the oven. We were truly blessed with her expert cooking and baking, which on occasion would win her a prize at WRI competition evenings.[2]

* * *

Months passed, and my message boy experiences blossomed. My work was varied and interesting, and I found that I

---

[2] Women's Rural Institute, formed in 1917 as the Scottish Rural Women's Institutes. In 2015 the organisation's name was changed to Scottish Women's Institutes.

learned something almost every day. Then, one Sunday in January after lunch, mum made an unexpected announcement.

"This is the year you leave school, so dad and I are going to take you and James on a special holiday in April," mum said as she tidied plates off the table.

"That's great, mum! Where are we going?" asked Peem.

"We're going to Jersey."

"Jersey! You mean Jersey in the Channel Islands? Wow!" Peem could hardly believe it.

"Jings! That's great. How will we get there?" I wondered.

"Dad? You'd better tell them," mum said as she brushed crumbs into a table dustpan.

"Well, like our London trip we did two years ago, I get free travel on the trains for me and mum. But it stops for you two after the age of fifteen. The Channel ferries are run by British Rail, so we'll get all our rail and ferry travel free."

"That's brilliant, dad!" I said in amazement.

"We'll get on a local train in Carnoustie then get on a fast train at Broughty Ferry all the way to London, and another train to Weymouth. Then we sail to Jersey."

"Your dad and I have got an insurance policy due to pay out, so that will pay for our boarding house in St Helier."

"What's St Helier?" asked Peem.

"That's the capital of Jersey," dad replied.

"Can I buy a new camera, mum?" I asked.

"Yes, you can take out some of your savings for your own pocket money for the whole holiday."

"Can I see a map, dad?" enquired Peem.

Dad opened the big family dictionary and turned to the back pages. We all had a look at the route and where the Channel Islands were.

"Gee," said Peem. "We'll nearly be in France!"

"I'll need to ask the school if you can have time off, but your exams won't have started by then so that should be alright," mum pointed out, adding: "You'll need to ask Mr Stewart for time off, Robert."

When Peem and I were in bed that night, we chatted about our great luck in holidaying in a place like Jersey.

"I dinna ken anybody in my class who's been out of Scotland," Peem said.

"Nor me. It's dad's job that makes it all possible, and it makes me wonder how many people make use of free passes to travel. We've been to London, and now Jersey. I'm beginning to think of a job on the railway."

There were lots of questions and plans, and at every opportunity Peem and I talked about what we might find in Jersey. We recalled the holiday we had in London two years previously, and wondered if the *Flying Scotsman* would be pulling our train again.

During that holiday, we had a four night long London visit where we visited Madame Tussaud's, the Tower of London, Buckingham Palace, and St Paul's Cathedral.

"Do you remember crawling along that ladder in St Pauls, Robbie?" Peem asked.

"I do! That was the scariest thing I've ever done in my life, and I'll never forget it."

"Do you think people are still allowed to do that?" he added.

"I very much doubt it."

He was referring to the day we climbed up the inside wooden steps to the top of St Paul's dome. A caretaker told us we could crawl along a horizontal ladder, resting on the wooden beams and plaster lathes, and peer from the top of the dome to the marble floor below.

"I don't think we'll do anything as dangerous as that in Jersey," I said.

Imagine a health and safety officer's reaction on learning of something so potentially dangerous happening today.

* * *

I continued to enjoy the shop environment, especially looking at the whole scene and to witness shop and window displays being set up. Sun shades were raised every day irrespective of the weather, powerful window lights switched on, and everything perfectly tidied. It seemed like a stage was prepared, waiting for the audience to arrive.

Above all, I enjoyed observing the friendly chat and bustling engagement with customers, whom I noticed could be grouped: school children sent with a shopping list inside a money-filled purse; elderly pensioners carefully spending every penny; and housewives doing family shopping. Often there were loud customers who liked telling jokes and stories. These were usually working men, sent with a list, and they seemed to enjoy having fun by teasing the staff.

At six o'clock the window lights were switched off, floors swept, and sunshades put away. The curtain was down again after another successful show.

* * *

With Isobel and Jean deposited with granny Taylor, we set off on our holiday to Jersey in late April.

"Have you got your pennies to throw out as we cross the Forth Bridge?" dad asked. "Remember: Grandad Murray said it was good luck."

Both Peem and I already had our pennies in our pockets, all set for the time-honoured lucky penny throw. We were sitting in a six-seat compartment and – when dad slid open the small window through which we threw our pennies – mum became quite upset as smoke and ashes from the engine swirled in, bringing not only dust but a smoky smell.

As we sat in our seats while stationary at Waverley Station, Edinburgh, dad told us an engine change was being made so we were all excited to eventually find out which special LNER (London and North East Railway) engine had been pulling us. As soon as he could, Peem ran ahead on King's Cross platform and came rushing back to tell us.

"Yes, it was the *Flying Scotsman*!"

As I walked past the engine, I could feel the heat from the boiler and steam was spurting out of pipes all around. The sheer power of the massive locomotive was awesome, and I could see how much the driver and fireman obviously enjoyed working on such a brilliant piece of engineering.

"Enjoy that, son?" asked the driver when he saw Peem's interest.

"Brilliant!" Peem replied, then turned to dad and said excitedly: "The driver spoke to me!"

It was a night of sailing, and we slept in two-tier bunks in a communal area for men and boys below deck. A strong breeze had created a swell and the ferry swayed about. But in the sleeping area it was warm and comfortable, spoiled only by a smell of oil and fumes, though we were so tired we quickly fell asleep. Mum and dad were somewhere in a cabin, and dad wakened us at nine o'clock in the morning to tell us we were arriving in St Peter's Port, Guernsey, en-route for Jersey. He asked if we wanted to see the ferry docking. Still half asleep, we emerged to a bright blue sky and a fresh salty sea breeze. We saw people and goods being moved about amongst a clatter and chatter of strange voices. I immediately felt the sun was warmer than back home in Westhaven, and enjoyed the first tinge of being in a foreign land as we sat on the open deck for the next step of the voyage to Jersey, marvelling at the following gulls above us.

Mum and dad organised visits to many places of inter-est, and I still remember the underground hospital, Elizabeth Castle, Gorey Castle (Mont Orgueil), the flower market and the Glass Church, all topped off with a bus trip around the island. Peem and I had a shock one afternoon while going for a walk along the rocky coastline. We kept walking into what was described, in white paint on a rock, as a 'naturist area'.

"This is great, Peem – we might see some interesting birds or animals here," I said, thinking we would have some-thing to write about someday in a school essay.

Just at that moment, as we were throwing stones into the sea, a naked man stood up – seemingly from nowhere – to wave his fist and shout at us.

"He must be a foreign nutcase," Peem observed.

But then, from various directions, several naked men and women immediately appeared from behind rocks. As we ran for our lives, we wondered why nobody was wearing clothes. We didn't tell mum and dad how we found it out, but that was the day we learned the difference between naturist and naturalist.

"Gee, that was a shock! We've had three big scares on our holidays now," Peem said as we walked back to our guest house.

"Well, I remember the St Paul's Dome adventure and now the Jersey beach mistake, but what was the third?"

"Don't tell me you've forgotten the time when you nearly fell down a well when we caravanned at Dunkeld?"

"Oh yes! That was more than a shock – that was a horror!"

Peem had reminded me of the time when we were collecting frogs at a caravan site on a farm near Dunkeld. Engrossed in pursuing a large green frog, I climbed over a fenced-off area around a well and carelessly stepped onto a large, cracked concrete slab sitting on top of the well. The slab was partially overgrown with grass, and one part of it gave way – as if hinged – when I stood on it. Luckily, my body weight was insufficient to make the slab fall – and me with it – into the water, which I could see a long way below. My feet slipped, and I was left trapped by the legs with the slab finely balanced to give way. I yelled as loud as I could, and Peem ran screaming for help. Men from the few caravans nearby came running, and one grabbed my shoulders while dad and the others pulled the slab away. With recurring nightmares of a precarious long drop into certain death, I found it difficult to sleep for a few nights. Just a boyhood scare – no stress-related syndrome in those days!

Just as we approached the guest house door, I warned: "Now remember, Peem – don't mention the naked people!"

It was a fantastic holiday, and I still have my prized photographs that I took with my new camera – but none of the naturist area.

* * *

"What's that you're reading, Peem?" I asked one evening.

"It's an advertisement for a Charles Atlas course."

I read the details, which promised ten easy steps to building a muscular body – along with a beach scene of a skinny boy having sand flicked on him by a well-built, good-looking boy.

"Why do you want to spend a lot of money on that? You're strong enough."

"I see all the money and tips you make, and I'm hoping to get a message bike job too."

"But Peem! I'm skinny, and I manage alright."

"Yes, but we could both do the course and share the cost – and the advert says you can attract good-looking girls if you have a muscular body."

"But why do you want to attract girls?"

"Well, the big lads from Carnoustie are coming to play catch and kiss at the ballaster, and I need to look stronger."

Peem was referring to the recent arrival of some bigger lads who were coming to Westhaven to play now that the old game of hide and seek had developed into catch and kiss. The Westhaven girls had friends from Carnoustie, and this had started to attract bigger boys who had heard of the adventures at the ballaster.

* * *

Behind the scenes at the end of each day I often overheard staff giggling about amusing mistakes made by customers and staff. It was hard work, but there was humour too which I shared. One little story related to Isobel, or Izzy as she liked to be called. Evidently, being so rushed off her feet she became confused while serving a customer. It happened like this. We sold bread which was meant to be 'slimming'. Its trade name was Nimble. We stocked both brown and white, and in her rush Izzy – when asked by her customer, Mrs Brown, for a Nimble – enquired: "Will that be a brown one, Mrs Nimble?"

Mrs Brown was an extremely fat lady, and the staff described her angry astonishment. Izzy was teased about this for days.

* * *

"Any report about Isobel's Dance Display evening?" asked dad as he opened the local *Guide and Gazette* newspaper one evening.

"It's on page four," mum said without looking up as she tidied the fireplace.

"Oh yes, here it is – 'Dazzling Dance Display'," dad read out. Peem and I were busy writing in our homework jotters, and dad was silent while he read the item and then he looked up. '...And special commendation to Isobel Murray for her perfect performances of Sailor's Hornpipe, Irish Washerwoman and the Highland Fling."

Isobel jumped up and down with excitement. She had taken part in her first ever end of term dancing display, and she blushed as we all applauded her success.

"Highland Games at Braemar next," teased Peem as he almost knocked over his ink pot.

"I couldn't have done it if the McLagans had never gone out," she joked.

Dad cut the article out of the *Guide and Gazette* and pasted it in his scrap book, where he kept all relevant family and extended family news.

* * *

One morning, when dad was having one of his regular rest days, an envelope was pushed through the letterbox. Mum had heard the postie coming up the stairs and grabbed the letter from behind the box.

"It's addressed to you, dad. Quickly; open the envelope, please. It looks like it's from the Council," mum urged as she leaned over dad's shoulder from behind his rocking chair.

He unfolded the letter and briefly studied it. "We're going to move on the 21st of this month," he said, the thrill in his voice unmistakeable. "That's only two weeks away!" dad added excitedly.

"Is that a definite date, dad?" asked mum as she continued to peer at the all-important document. "After all those years of waiting?"

"Well, it's all here in print from the Council," Dad responded, his voice calming.

"Read on, dad. Tell us where we're going," mum said emotionally as she danced around the room.

"You'll have to have a guess," he teased.

"Holyrood Street?" called out Peem.

"Primrose Street?" I ventured.

"Come on then, mum," said dad. "I know what you want."

"Oh, I'm hoping, but I'll not get my first choice."

Dad passed her the letter and she quickly scanned it.

"Well I never! That's my dream come true! Three bed-rooms," mum shrilled.

"Tell us!" we all called out.

"It's Shamrock Street. Number four. But we'll need to get our skates on – we've only got two weeks before we move in. Dad, you'll need to try and get time off. We'll have to get keys and see how much work has to be done on it."

That morning as I went to school, I remember thinking the long bike run in all weathers from Westhaven to school would end. It didn't take long for a pang of regret to emerge. Life in Westhaven – a wonderful gem – would be over, and I would be jettisoned into the town. What would it be like?

The next Sunday was special, as we all realised it was going to be the last time we would walk over the Steenie Brig to church from Anchor Place. Mum had said we would have a lunch later than usual and so, on the way home from church, I asked if I could have a look at the harbour. Boats were moored in the normal way, and the tide looked like it was on the way in. It was at the exact stage where Jim used to commence his boat-minding duties. I sat on a bench and watched cormorants drying their wings while perched on harbour poles. My thoughts went back to the glorious days I had spent with Jim when he looked after boats for the fisher-men.

I can still picture the line of well-known boats which Jim helped to look after. The smallest was *Grace*, moored alongside the long, sleek, blue-and-cream-coloured *Osprey*. Where deeper water was needed were the green *Sea Hawk* (the ex-lifeboat) and *Meta*, painted dark brown with a green interior.

Most of his duties were for Mr Clark, owner of *Grace* – the same man who ran the cycle shop and looked after my message bike. He regularly sailed a twelve-foot clinker-built cobble which he had built himself. On a designated day and time, Jim's task was to wait for the tide to reach the boat and – with the water up to his knees – undo the warps, step into the boat, and sail around wherever he wished until Mr Clark appeared ready to go fishing. Jim would then row the boat to the shore and hand over the cobble. Without someone like Jim, the boat would have been inaccessible in deep water on its moorings.

As I sat there looking at the harbour, I saw the *Sea Hawk* – a larger fishing boat (Jim said it was previously a ship's lifeboat) owned by a few men – and vividly recalled the day Jim asked us to help him. He followed the same procedure and, once the boat was free from its moorings, had us aboard.

"Jump in, lads. Peem and Coffie, you sit at the stern. Robbie, you and Ollie sit at the bow. Peem, hold on to these rowlocks."

While we sorted ourselves out, Jim pulled out two oars which had been tucked under the seats and sat in the centre seat facing the stern. "Put these rowlocks in there, Peem," he instructed, indicating the centre points of the boat. Jim was in charge, and took his responsibilities seriously. I remember he negotiated his way out of the harbour and – rowing against the tide – we were soon out in the open sea with cold sea-water spraying my back.

"It's a braw day, boys, and we've got twa 'oors tae hae a wee sail."

None of us had the strength of Jim. We instinctively trusted his skills, and felt comfortable under his leadership. Nevertheless, it was quite scary once out in unprotected waters with the swell of a rising tide. We sailed past platforms of ducks and floats of sea gulls. I faced the shore and took in a totally new view of Westhaven when Coffie called out in alarm: "What was that?"

"What did you see?" asked Jim.

"I don't know! A big black thing, like a seal or a whale."

"That'll be a porpoise or a dolphin. They're safe enough; dinna worry."

Now and again a pod of dolphins or porpoises would emerge and swim alongside us, and after some time Jim shipped the oars and had a rest, allowing the boat to wallow in the swell.

"Should have had our fishing lines with us," Peem suggested.

"You're right, but we need different lines out here. We'll do that the next time," Jim replied.

Our exciting adventure continued for another hour or so while Jim told us many tales of scares he had experienced, and we were in awe of his single-handed abilities. Then we turned for the shore. Jim tidied up the boat, got us all off, and within minutes the fishermen were ready to board.

Deep in thought, I was trying to recall the names of the men when I was interrupted by Isobel.

"Mum sent me along to see if you are alright," she said. "Lunch is ready; you need to come now."

I remember it was a sad lunch time as I recalled those wonderful adventures. The other end of Carnoustie was going to be like an entirely new world.

* * *

Our Sunday routine was at an end, and we chatted about how things would change. Great excitement followed, and I couldn't wait for the move to our new house. On a few occasions during the next several days I cycled past on my message bike to have a look at number four, and tried to imagine what life was going to be like inside. It looked huge, with a garden at the front and rear and a back door – and a front door!

It was strange to think that my message bike job had seen the end of my Westhaven world as I had known it, and now this move would take us away from the Ha'en altogether. That was sad. We all felt the same about moving away, but to have a three-bedroomed house with a kitchen and bathroom (complete with a bath) all to ourselves, as well as a garden, was a luxury. Mum and dad had been to the house and, later, we all did little bits of cleaning and tidying. Furniture vans were expensive, dad had said, so we moved on the 21st – a dry day – with the aid of a flat-bed lorry. Dad and mum had travelled to Shamrock Street in the lorry with their bikes on top. Isobel walked home from school, and Peem and I cycled to our new home. I hadn't had a thrill like this since the first day I moved from Annfield Cottage to Admiral Street. Oddly, the first thing we missed was the wash house, so all our bikes had to be covered by tarpaulin.

"We'll need to speak to your brother Jim and ask if he can make a shed for us," dad suggested to mum. "A winter will cause a lot of damage."

A flurry of activity – curtains, linoleum, carpets, painting and decorating – had everyone busy. We were each given tasks, and mum and dad had to make a long-term plan to get the house the way they wanted it.

"The garden's covered in weeds," bemoaned dad. "The only thing I can plant in there, next year, is tatties. But that'll help to clean the ground."

Peem and I shared a bigger bedroom with a spacious built-in wardrobe and a large window which overlooked the garden. Isobel and Jean shared their own room, while mum and dad – for the first time since 1944 – had a bedroom of their own. We were all excited, and I imagined mum and dad were pleased after they had waited so long to be allocated a Council house they were to enjoy. Mum, in the end, got her first choice. With four children aged from fourteen months to fourteen years in a two-bedroom flat with no bathroom, they deserved it. My message bike job kept me busy, and I found myself cycling around that part of the town where I now lived. A lot easier to call in for a jacket or pullover and a bite to eat.

Adventures on my rounds continued. One evening when I returned to the shop – soaking wet, having been caught without waterproofs in a heavy downpour – the boss said to me with a grin: "Are you sure you're still enjoying this, Robert?"

"Yes, but my mum thinks I'm silly. She'll tell me off to-night when I have to be dried out!"

This was followed by the boss's humorous chant, which I now thought I had analysed.

* * *

There was one matter, though, that didn't make the boss so happy. It concerned the jolly and chatty Mrs Rigg, who lived in the property above the shop. While pushing up the sun-shades one evening, I witnessed the problem. It was about two minutes to six o'clock when, wearing her pink slippers, she hurriedly passed me and trotted into the shop. I overheard her request – directed to the boss, who had just finished cleaning the meat machine.

"Four ounces of luncheon meat cut thin, please."

It was a perfectly pleasant request, but the problem was that the boss would then have to clean the machine again. For me it was a lesson in excellent customer service, for the boss smiled as he cut the wafer-thin slices. As he did so, he hummed a tune which I eventually recognised as his "Go, go, greasy grocer go" phrase.

Was this his way of covering up his anger while providing a cheery service – and at the same time giving himself some fun? After Mrs Rigg had gone, he said: "It's a strange thing. In all my years in the trade, I've found the customers who live nearest are always the ones who dash in at the last minute."

I didn't know if there was truth in that statement, but I'd been aware of staff comments about a Mrs Rigg. Now I had seen the problem and, from then onwards, I kept an eye open. Once I came back from a late delivery to find the blinds down and Mrs Rigg inside the shop waiting for her usual four ounces cut thin. The boss didn't look quite so happy, but he was still humming!

* * *

Christmas 1954 was, for me, a repeat of the previous year – but I was prepared for the hectic life on the bike. The boss asked me to do all the usual things: clear out the tomato boxes for Freddy, bring down last year's stock of unsold crackers, and work full time for two weeks. Again, my tips excelled and my can filled up. It was time to count my earnings and look in to see Miss Black in the New Year. I cycled my way around the streets whistling the top songs of the time, and the two I remember were 'I Saw Mummy Kissing Santa Claus' and the Eddie Calvert trumpet tune 'Oh Mein Papa'.

One evening I was whistling in full tune when I met Jock.

"Here's whistling Robbie," he called out. "You must be happy!"

"Yes, Jock," I replied. "Best Christmas ever!"

I'd had only two and wasn't sure if it was, but I said it anyway as my method of trying to keep ahead of Jock before he boasted of his 'best quality' hams, cheeses, wines or spirits.

* * *

In July 1955 the pupils in my class, being fifteen years old, were permitted to leave school at the start of the summer holiday. It was Friday the 4th of July, our last day together as a class, when we trooped off to the Beach Hall to receive our Leaving Certificates. It was our big day, with mixed feelings of satisfaction, excitement and nervousness about the future. I sat sandwiched between my school friends Bill McGregor and Willie Yool, who were both at least six months older than me. When the moment arrived, Bill eagerly leapt up to collect his certificate and the school dux prize, and shortly after Willie proudly walked up to receive the prize in technical subjects. For my second-in-the-class place, I received the leaving certificate and my chosen prize: a book entitled *The Rustlers of Rattlesnake Valley* which I'm quite sure caused outrage in the staffroom. The truth of the matter was that I was given a maximum sum of ten shillings and sixpence (fifty-two and a half pence) to spend in the local bookshop and, although I searched for something genuinely educational, there was nothing within that price range. I recall that in a rare burst of rebellion I chose my contentious prize book, and I can still to this day see the grimace on the headmaster's face as he handed it over.

Bill – one of the younger members of his family of thirteen – excelled, and had already secured a job in the Royal Bank of Scotland, while Willie was ready to start the following Monday as a joinery apprentice. I remember feeling completely lost and bereft of any ideas for my future.

After the ceremony I asked each of my teachers for their autograph and Miss Main, our geography teacher, wrote in my book: "Independence Day – Good Luck!" However, it was not for me – my 15th birthday would be in October, and myself and three others had to continue until the start of the two-week October holiday. If there had been no such holiday, I would have remained at school until Christmas. The arrangement between the farmers and the Scottish Education Department allowed pupils in certain designated farming areas to be released for a two-week holiday (the 'Tattie Holidays') to assist with gathering the potato crop.

All my other classmates started work that summer and one of them, Alan Craigie – who made his own basic radios in his bedroom – commenced as a radio and TV apprentice, which I thought was a clever choice. Mathematics, trigonometry, algebra and geometry had been enjoyable, and I consistently obtained top marks. Television sets were beginning to appear in homes, and I also thought television and radio work would be interesting career.

Nearly all my friends were now in jobs where they had Saturday off and enjoyed a long weekend break. When on my message bike I saw them out and about in the town enjoying themselves with trips to football matches in Dundee, I felt I was missing something.

A few weeks after the summer holiday I saw, by chance, an advertisement in a local paper for an apprentice radio and TV mechanic with Reekie, an engineering company based in Arbroath. Eventually, accompanied by mum and clutching my school certificates, I attended an interview.

"Do you know the difference between linking batteries in series or in parallel?" was one of the questions asked by Mr Ford, the senior manager. Luckily that subject had been my most recent science lesson and, like me, he must have been surprised by my crystal-clear answer. Two weeks later I was offered the job, which would start as soon as I left school.

I'd been near the top of my class when I was twelve, but didn't progress to high school as mum said she couldn't afford all of us to go. There were classmates who were below me in class who did go to high school, and this gave me a feeling of being cheated as I considered I had the ability. Now I was fifteen years old and had to leave. At the school gates on my last day I vividly recall taking one big step across an imaginary line at the exit and saying to myself: "Well, here I go. I don't want to leave school, but where else can I go?"

Now it was my time to tell the new message boy – who looked as nervous as I probably had on day one – about boxes, tyres, lights, and parking on level ground.

"Remember, David – the boss doesn't like spending money on batteries."

It seemed only a few months previously when I'd been told that. He wouldn't have to deal with mice and maggots, but he would have to find out about collecting lettuce, delivering to the jam factory and Soldier's Home, and all the other rigours like carrying in half a ton of sugar. That was for him to experience.

"Oh, just one more thing, David. I'll lower the seat two or three inches for you."

Seemed like yesterday when Freddie did the same for me. I must have secretly grown. I wished him luck, and took my woodwork apron home to be washed for the last time. Jock had left school in July and was now an apprentice grocer; when I met him in the street, I told him my decision.

"Can't stand the pace, eh?"

"It's the job of the future, Jock."

As I said that, I had a hollow feeling that I was leaving something I enjoyed, yet I believed that I had to go out into a new technical world and use my mathematical skills.

The staff wished me luck, and the boss joked: "So the wee greasy grocer's away to be a sparky!"

What an extremely eventful year it had been!

CHAPTER 12

A New World, or "Redheads are Not Allowed on Boats!"

Spring 1956

AS an apprentice TV engineer, I was kitted out in navy blue dungarees. At ten past seven on cold dark October mornings – except Sundays – I was on my way to Arbroath in a bus full of cigarette smokers. Each evening I returned home around six thirty, except on half-day Saturdays when I finished at one o'clock.

Having my usual soup and pudding lunch in a small café, I unexpectedly found myself briefly reunited with my classmates from 1952. They now wore the green uniform of Arbroath High School, and all appeared to be enjoying themselves. Secretly, I wished I could be with them.

Most days in my new job I was out and about in a small Ford van helping nineteen year old apprentice Bob to lift heavy TV sets. Some were new, being delivered and installed in homes. Others were collected for repair. With a mattress in the back of the van on which the sets were laid, Bob drove like a maniac all around Angus town and country roads. This was a totally different, hair-raising world for me.

One of my jobs was to take new sets out of their packaging and set them up for test runs. TV sets were selling well, and I was kept busy. Fishing families in the town lived in an area near the harbour referred to as the 'Fit o' the Toon', and they were by far the biggest spenders. They bought only the top-range console models in walnut or mahogany cabinets. I calculated that farmers were in second place.

"Another 'trauchle' up narrow stairs today, Robbie," said Bob. He was referring to the fact that fishing families preferred their TV sets upstairs in a small lounge. They seemed very well-off people, and their terraced homes were compact and immaculate.

My last task of the day was to top up customers' radio batteries with acid and distilled water, then link them up to the charger. Mr Ford's interview question was certainly relevant.

A long bench in the workshop typically had around four or five TVs and some radios under repair. The back covers of sets had been removed and tools, wires, components, screws and washers were cluttered around each set. Constant whistling noises from radios and music from the 1950s TV screen test card filled the air, accompanied by the smell of flux and heat from the permanently switched-on soldering irons.

Some radios and TVs were test run for days, even weeks.

"It's a slow process of elimination," said Ernie, one of the three senior engineers when I enquired about the sets lined up on the bench.

"Some faults are intermittent, so we have to run them 'til we've cured the problem."

Once a set was repaired, I was often asked to attach the back cover.

Occasionally an engineer would ask me to pass him a valve – for example, a PR3, a WH80, a VHF condenser, or perhaps an R12 resistor. Every resister had a specific value which was designated by its colour code, and each component had a code number. My job was to select a labelled item from the spares cabinet, then hand it over. Not much more technical than handling cans of soup or beans!

One perk of working in the workshop, surrounded by radios, was that the current top songs were invariably heard – mainly because Bob tuned in to them whenever he got the chance. I remember 'Rock around the Clock' was blasted out, often closely followed by 'Autumn Leaves'. Bob was a whistler, like myself, and was in great tune nearly all day – especially as he drove madly around – but for some reason I had stopped my tunes. Perhaps it was the fact I couldn't compete with Bob, or that I wasn't pedalling along on my message bike.

Davie, another senior engineer, was a really busy livewire, and an authority on fishing boat radios and echo sounders.

"You can come with me sometime and see what goes on," he said one day while filling his bags with tools and spare parts.

"Brilliant! I'll look forward to that," I said with glee.

A few days later, Davie enthusiastically announced: "Grab your jacket, Robbie my boy! We're off to the harbour."

He asked me to stand beside the van while he went aboard a seine net boat, which was moored and lying against the harbour wall beside some stone steps.

"Bring down my bag of spares, Robbie boy," he cried up to me. As I was about to step down towards him, Davie called again. "Stay where you are, Robbie! I'll come up and get them," he said.

I was curious, and I soon found out why when we finally sat in the van ready to go back to the workshop.

"Couldn't get you on board, my boy. I've been reminded that redheads are not allowed on boats. It's bad luck."

"Why is that?"

"It's a superstition. Something to do with Vikings."

I couldn't believe what the Vikings had done, approximately seven hundred years previously, had effectively ruined my prospects of having a career in boats' radios and echo sounders.

One day in the street I met Jim.

"Don't see you around these days."

"No, I'm in Arbroath doing radio and TV work."

As soon as I replied, I was aware it sounded rather grand and untrue – because in reality, I was a 'go for', a battery filler, a van assistant, and I handed over components to engineers.

"Oh, I thought you liked the Willie Low job."

"Yes, I do," I responded, immediately noticing that I hadn't said "did".

Because I'd had to stay on at school until October, I was one year late in getting to technical college for my day release classes in radio engineering. By the time the next college year started, I'd have lost a year and be nearly sixteen years old. A year then seemed a huge disadvantage.

* * *

I didn't know for certain at the time, but the Scout camp of 1953 was my last. There was no leader to organise a camp in 1954, and consequently attendance numbers at the usual Tuesday meetings dwindled. I was still a Scout, but didn't attend all meetings. My preoccupation with leaving school and impending work plans took my mind off enthusiastically working for more badges as I had once done. My last Scout attendance was to be part of the War Memorial parade in November. It was a cold, raw day with a strong wind whipping up dead leaves in the road, and by the time we had assembled in our shorts and marched to the memorial gardens I was frozen. I had always been aware that my dad's brother, my uncle Jim, had been killed at El Alamein when he was twenty one years old, and that was one strong reason why I wanted to take part.

Mum told me that my uncle – a soft-spoken, well-mannered young man – had an unexpected forty-eight hours leave, and had travelled from Montrose to Barry in the hope of meeting them prior to him returning to England to set sail in the early summer of 1942. Unfortunately dad's shift didn't allow him to meet his brother. Evidently Jim ruffled my hair, said I was a bonny wee carrot head, and put a shilling in my hand for good luck. He was killed on the first night of the battle, and mum showed me a letter she'd sent to him but which had been returned as he died before receiving it. I have always felt a close affinity with uncle Jim, and felt for my dad who missed out on saying goodbye to his brother.

My winter was spent doing routine and unskilled jobs. Being too eager to learn, and knowing I had a long wait for technical college training to start, I became frustrated. Acid splashes resulted in replacing two pairs of dungarees. It would be six months – or two more dungarees – before I could start college.

"Why do you get splashes like that?" asked mum nearly every week. "Don't you get an apron?"

As a message boy I'd been earning thirteen and sixpence a week plus tips, giving me over one pound per week. My pay was now one pound and ten shillings weekly, minus the cost of bus fares and lunches. No longer was I able to regularly hand over ten shillings to mum, as my net pay was only a few shillings. Peem was planning to go to art school and he wouldn't be contributing to the household income, Isobel was still at school, and Jean was only three years old. This served to remind me how tight money was at home. To save a few shillings each week and be nearer my work, I started to travel by train and leave my bike at the station. It was quick and easy, as it wasn't necessary in those days to chain or lock up my bike when I parked.

While cycling home one Monday evening in spring 1956, I saw the lights still switched on in Willie Lows. I hadn't discussed anything with mum and dad, nor had I decided when I would do it, but on impulse I parked my bike and knocked on the front door and pictured the scene: the boss would be there, counting cash.

"Can I come back and work here, Mr Stewart?" I blurted out as soon as he opened the door.

"You'd better come in," he said. "What's wrong with you?"

"I'm not learning anything in Arbroath. I'd be happier back here. Could I get a full-time job?

"I'll need to ask Munro, but I'm sure it'll be okay. Look in and see me on Thursday. Don't hand in your notice yet. There's a young lad meant to be transferring from Dundee to me next week."

"Thanks."

I went home, praying the transfer could be stopped. A job for me was not guaranteed, but luckily the boss must feel that he needs help. Fingers crossed.

Continuing to work with my engineering colleagues, having secretly made an enquiry about leaving them, was not pleasant. What's more, there were some occasions when one of the engineers would take time to explain something technical to me which also made me feel a cheat. Some days were enjoyable, and I began to develop self-doubts about my intention to leave. Was I making the right decision? Would I have to return to Mr Stewart and say it was all my mistake? My mind was in a whirl about the move. Could I hold out? There were moments when I could have gone in either direction. After an anxious three days, I stopped off to get the boss's answer.

"I've had a word with Munro and you can start a week on Monday."

"Oh, that's great!" I said with undisguised relief.

As I cycled home, I found myself whistling for the first time in many long months and the current tune was 'Cherry Pink and Apple Blossom White' – a melody I have always associated with that moment. It was as if I'd had a bad dream and was now waking up safely. I went home and revealed my secret to mum.

"Well, if you're sure. Do you really want to do that?"

"I'm not enjoying the job in Arbroath."

"Alright then, if you think you'll manage."

Mum's usual guiding words. I didn't tell her it was anything to do with not giving her ten shillings a week, but hoped I could be able to start that again.

"We'll speak about it later, Robert," she said. "Tonight is my annual visit to see the Musical Society show."

Mum saved up all year for her treat, and I didn't want to delay her. But I was relieved she had made no comment about me not being sure about my future.

After tea, I went upstairs and found Peem trying to come to grips with chords to play 'The Ballad of Davy Crockett' on his second-hand guitar. Before long, I was whistling along with him.

Next day, with a clear mind, I gave the required one week's notice. The truth of the matter was that Saturday afternoons off were not so important as previously thought. I'd lost contact with my school pals and, in any case, had no money to attend football matches or shop in Dundee. More than that, I was aware that I had no rapport with valves, resisters and condensers. The prospect of waiting until next winter to start technical training was gloomy, and my pal Alan Craigie was already repairing sets. The reality was that the slow, painstaking process of dealing with intermittent technical faults was at loggerheads with my personality and temperament. My pace of life and work was brisk. Luckily, I had some sense to recognise that I missed the stage, the vibrancy of the show, and the clamour and excitement of the shop buzz.

The boss's "Go, Go, Greasy Grocer Go" oft-coined phrase was in tune with me. I can't prove it and I didn't think of it at the time, but cycling past the shop each evening perhaps had a magnetic influence. What would have happened if I'd kept travelling by bus?

An indication of my desire to return was the fact that I didn't ask the boss what my weekly pay would be, but I was sure it would likely be better. When I received my first pay packet I found it was two pounds twelve and sixpence. Big money, and once more I could help mum. Arriving early in the familiar environment on my first day the boss announced: "See if that'll fit you." It was a white coat.

"Oh yes, that's fine," he said. "You look like a real greasy grocer after all."

My grocery apprenticeship had begun. You've no idea what you started, Jim.

CHAPTER 13

Now an Apprentice Grocer, or "Chocolate Vermicelli, Please"

Autumn 1956

"BE home early tonight now, Robert, because Isobel is bringing home her first cooked meal that she's made at school," mum said as I prepared to set off to work after lunch.

"What will the meal be?"

"It's a surprise. But I've promised her we'll all be here to sample her food," mum added as she tidied away my lunch plates from the kitchen table.

Isobel was in her first senior year, and had been cooking at school for some weeks. Along with her classmates, they had already provided a range of dishes including rice pudding, mince and potatoes, and a beef stew. I rushed home and was last to arrive; the rest of the family were poised waiting for the latest delicacy. Plates and cutlery were already on the table, and Isobel – complete with mum's apron – opened the oven door and brought out a large bowl of soup.

"It was cooled on the way home, so I had to heat it up. Let's hope it's alright," she said in a new-found, mature manner. We were each given a ladle of her school-made soup.

"What kind of soup is it?" asked Peem.

"It's chicken and vegetable," Isobel replied. "Do you like it?" she enquired, standing back to await comments.

"It's excellent," said dad as he licked his spoon. "When are we going to open our own café?"

"So we have a dancer who is also a cook in the family now," mum remarked as she laid out more plates.

Mum presented us with a main dish of beef stew, potatoes and vegetables, and we all tucked in.

"Did anybody notice anything different with the meal tonight?" she asked.

None of us had any answers. But then Isobel called out: "I made it!"

It transpired that mum had said to Isobel that the next time she came home with a soup, mum would allow her to make the main meal. Isobel was grinning from ear to ear. It was her first meal we had tasted, and she was proud of her achievement.

"Isobel is going to make one meal a week for us from now on, and all the boys will do the washing up," said mum.

Dad, Peem and I looked at each other and tried to smile.

"Will we have to work in the café too?" asked Peem with genuine concern.

It was all fun, and it gave Isobel a lot of confidence for her future cooking at school.

"You and James will have to sleep in a tent this year," mum announced as she peeled potatoes at the kitchen sink one Sunday morning.

"What?" asked a confused Peem as he looked up from reading The Broons in the *Sunday Post*.

"Are we going away on holiday somewhere?" I added.

"No. I've loaned a tent so that you and James can sleep in the back garden when the Taylors and Christies are here."

"What happens if it rains?" Peem queried.

"Don't worry. We still have all your camp sleeping bags and groundsheets, and I'll waken you in the morning. You'll get your breakfast before our visitors are up."

When I first heard mum's plan I felt embarrassed that our neighbours would think we were becoming tinkers, but as the idea grew I became less troubled.

"The families won't be here at the same time, but it will mean each family will have two bedrooms rooms and I'll be able to charge a little bit more this year. They were all cramped in one bedroom last year."

Looking back, I could see mum was well-organised and could probably have run a boarding house or hotel. She worked hard all day, providing three meals to our and family and guests, and seemed to enjoy producing her favourite dishes. In those days families from all over the central belt of Scotland loved the fresh sea breezes and the clean beaches, resulting in places like Carnoustie witnessing a doubling or almost trebling of the population. Mum and dad began to introduce the summer visitors to walks around the countryside, and enjoyed joint picnics and trips with them. Each year Charles continued to enjoy fishing, and his cousin Gilbert in time followed suit. Mary, Gilbert's big sister, was a lovely girl and Mrs Christie made it clear she was keen for me to ask her out. Isobel and Mary became close friends, but somehow I never plucked up the courage to invite Mary on a date as I thought she was too young for me.

In time mum stopped charging for accommodation, and food costs were shared. Somehow the unfortunate Mr Christie – who was a skilled carpenter – was, during his holiday, volunteered by his wife to do joinery jobs around the house as payment, and made many improvements over the years. The paying guests became lifetime friends, and connections with both families remain to this day. Mrs Christie was a jolly, rosy-cheeked farmer's wife figure, and she told me the story behind her husband's unfortunate deafness. When still children, he and his two sisters had their tonsils removed by a doctor while – one at a time – they lay anaesthetised on their kitchen table. This resulted in three deaf children. Now we know why we have a National Health Service!

* * *

On a visit to the bank one morning, while wearing my white, starched shop coat, I met Jock.

"Whose house are you painting?" he asked cheekily, nodding in the direction of my white coat.

Seeing him for the first time in his short khaki jacket, I said: "New legislation for hygienic grocers. By the way, where's your joinery job this morning?"

"So you're back in the grocery trade? Haven't seen you for a long time. How did the sparky job go?"

Not wishing to go into detail, I casually declared: "Oh, I decided to come back and steal your customers."

"Away you go! You'll never do that, Robbie."

"Just wait and see."

Uncharacteristically, he was stuck for an answer. But I knew he'd bounce back.

* * *

An immediate change was noticeable in the pace of learning new parts of the business. Working in the front shop area became normal, where I was permitted to build displays. Now I was required not only to merely prepare stock, but to replenish every section. One day the boss said: "It's about time you started serving at the counter and give us help at busy times."

"I'm not too sure about using the bacon machine and the meat slicer."

"Right, I'll show you when we're closed tonight. Bacon machine first."

The boss gave me thorough instructions on how to set thickness of slices, cutting, weighing, pricing and cleaning, with great emphasis on safety. He also gave me the rules on how, in his words, to 'work away' fatty pieces.

"It's money, remember. I had to pay for these bad bits."

After a few practice runs, he seemed pleased with my progress.

"Now, let's deal with the meat slicer. Same principles."

The best time I imagined I could venture towards a customer was when it was quiet, early in the week or just before closing time, and when help was at hand if required. My opportunity, I felt, would be in some weeks away. But my chance came sooner than I'd imagined.

On the following Monday, when there were no other customers in the shop, Cathie gave the command. I'll never forget her words.

"Right, Robert. You're serving the next customer to come through the door."

"Oh, gee!"

A few minutes later, who should appear but Miss Fleming – my unsmiling, one-time science teacher.

"Oh no!" I blurted out. But a prod in my back by Cathie propelled me forward. Nervously, I edged into the unknown.

"Hello, Miss Fleming."

"Well, well. It's you, Robert Taylor Murray."

"Yes, Miss."

I was about to know some secrets of one of my teachers, and I trembled. What food does she like? Or what quality of butter will she buy? It was a strange feeling.

"Two pounds of sugar please, Robert."

Now this teacher needed me after all those years. *Sugar's easy. Phew! So, she doesn't buy Jock's posh West Indian cane sugar.*

"Quarter pound of tea."

"Which one, Miss?"

"Oh, the 1/3d one, please."

Gee, she buys the cheapest tea.

"You're not in school now, Robert. It's Miss Fleming."

"Oh! Yes. Sorry, Miss."

She laughed at my mistake. Wow, I'd had a joke with Miss Fleming. My stern science teacher.

"Now some biscuits, please. Half a pound."

"Yes. What kind would you like?"

Pulling a bag off the string, I walked to the rack of biscuit tins with glass lids.

"Oh, just a mixture."

Wow, Miss Fleming's going to eat biscuits I've touched, and I'm going to decide which ones she'll eat.

And then: "A quarter of ******, please."

I paused. Whatever she'd said to me was utterly incomprehensible.

Things had been going well. But... what?

"Ferm-eh-selli? Sorry, Miss," I stammered.

Dumbstruck, I wanted to fall into a hole and never come out.

"You *do* stock it, Robert."

"I don't think we have..."

Cathie came to the rescue.

"Here, Robert. Chocolate vermicelli is here," she said, pulling out a small drawer behind the counter. I'd seen the stuff before, but didn't know its name. So now I knew.

I weighed a quarter pound.

"Anything more, Miss Fleming?"

"No, that's fine, thank you."

The next test. To total the amount. The practise was that strips of blank paper were routinely kept on the counter, and all I had to do was list the cost of each item on a slip. I'd seen how it was done – write the price, then move the items one at a time to the other side of me. Totalling the sum, but before uttering anything, I asked Cathie to check.

"Yes, that's right, Robert."

"That's four and sixpence please, Miss Fleming."

She fumbled in her purse and handed me a ten shilling note. I registered the sum on the till, put the note in the till, and handed her five and sixpence change. She put her bag on the rail, and I passed over each item. As she packed her bag she enquired: "Are you enjoying your work here?"

"Yes, Miss Fleming – and you're my first customer."

She had probably spotted my nervousness, but merely said: "Well done. Thank you, Robert."

Then she nodded and smiled to Cathie.

"Thank you, too"

She closed the shop door behind her.

"Phew! That's not the Miss Fleming I knew at school. She's really very friendly," I said to Cathie.

"That was a good start, Robert," Cathie observed.

"But I felt so daft about the fermi... what do call it again?"

"Chocolate vermicelli."

"I'll know the next time."

"Look, Robert – all those cake decorations are in these shallow drawers."

Cathie pulled out two drawers.

"Those are what we call the coupon drawers."

"Why are they called that?"

"Because during the war, customers had to have ration books to buy meat, cheese, tea, and so on. Depending on family circumstances they could only buy if they had enough coupons.

"I've never seen any coupons."

"No, that's all stopped now. Customers each had ration books and could only buy what they were allocated. They were last used a year or two ago."

Another piece of learning for me.

"I'm still shaking," I said to Cathie just as Dot and Izzy put their heads around the corner from the back shop.

"You'll never forget chocolate vermicelli all your life now!" laughed Izzy. She was right.

"We were praying for you," said Dot.

Cathie added an instruction.

"Remember: always put the money you get on top of the till. Then count the change back into the customer's hand. Don't just hand over coins. Only then do you put the money you get into the till drawer."

"Why put money on top of the till?"

"It proves what you received from the customer, and stops any misunderstandings."

"Gee, I'm glad you were with me, Cathie."

"We all had to start at some stage. Always ask if you're not sure about something."

The boss put his head around from the back shop. He'd probably been listening too.

"How did he do, then?" he said with a grin.

"Fine," I said weakly.

"We'll make a greasy grocer of you yet, then!"

When I went home that evening, I thought about Miss Fleming. It was the fact that I now had private information about her. There was a need for trust. She wouldn't want me to reveal her decisions. I wouldn't be telling my pals. It was my first lesson in customer confidentiality. It was something I'd never thought about before.

"I served my first customer today," I told mum as I sat down at the kitchen table.

"Oh? How did you get on?"

"Fine. It was Miss Fleming."

"Your teacher? My goodness! Were you nervous?"

"Yes, but it was all okay."

I remember thinking that I now knew something about Miss Fleming, but couldn't tell mum. The feeling was loyalty to my customer.

As I lay in bed that evening, another thought struck me. Now I know for certain why I left the radio and TV job. It's people I like, not valves and resisters. Each day's experiences helped me to reaffirm that.

Thanks yet again, Jim. It was you who started it all.

From that day on I was gradually able to serve more customers. The experienced staff always 'worked it' so that I didn't get a difficult customer. I must admit, I tried in the beginning to 'pick out' ladies who would have small purchases, but the easiest customers were children sent with shopping lists.

I couldn't wait to tell Jock about my counter experiences.

CHAPTER 14

Real Progress, or "How to Make a Streaky Roll"

Autumn 1956

SERVING customers became a large part of my work. Every Saturday and most of Fridays, all staff – including myself – were working almost constantly at the counter.

It became clear that queues lengthened if stock was not ready to hand. David – the new message boy – replenished the fast-selling items, just as I had done.

We took turns to have a rushed cup of tea. Of course, I was last. Real pressure prevented taking even one extra second over the five minute break. Often the boss would say, during my rest period, something like: "Put another butter on the slab, Robert, when you're ready! Go, go, greasy..." His chant tailing away as he rushed to the back shop. My interpretation of this statement was that my tea break was now over. It was not unusual to see more than one half-consumed cup of tea abandoned in the back shop.

One day on my way to John Yool's grocery shop to exchange a can of Mock Turtle soup, I met Jock.

"Are you going to evening classes in August?" he asked.

"Don't know yet."

I'd heard about grocery classes in Dundee, but because it would involve getting away early from work I hadn't plucked up the courage to ask the boss.

More new jobs were designated to me, and cleaning and sharpening the bacon and cooked meat machines became routine – when total concentration was required with no distractions.

"We don't want any ambulances!" was the boss's constant reminder.

* * *

"Right, Robert – a new job," Mr Stewart said one quiet afternoon. "Time to show you how to make a streaky roll."

"Oh, a streaky! I've seen you do that."

"Well, it's time you learned. Now, the whole point of making a streaky is to prevent loss."

"What do you mean?"

"Have you seen all those fatty bacon ends that are too small to cut on the machine?"

"Yes."

"Well, we can't just throw them out, can we? It's all money!"

"Yes – a bit like the tomato boxes and biscuit tins."

"You're learning! So, let me tell you. I buy two sides of streaky bacon every week."

He laid the two flat pieces on the bench. Each piece was about two feet long, nine inches wide – tapering to about six – and roughly two or three inches thick.

"First, you put one streaky skin down and put all the fatty pieces along the top of it. Then you lay the other skin up on top, and sandwich the fatty ends between the two long pieces. Like this."

He then tied string around it every three inches or so along its length, forming the whole thing up into a long roll and creating a neat line of knots as he did so. As he tied each string, he told me: "This is a slip knot which won't come undone. It's called a 'kinch'."

He left a few spaces along the roll, and I guessed what he was about to say.

"Now you try it."

I had a go, and soon found it easier than I had thought.

"Just make sure the kinch is as tight as possible. Now there you are, Robert. You'll make a streaky roll next week."

"I'll try!"

"We'll make a greasy grocer of you yet," he laughed.

Under his supervision the following week, I managed to make one. Apart from the boss tightening one or two kinches, he said it was fine. Another first.

"You'll make the streaky rolls every week now."

* * *

One day the boss and all the staff were serving customers when, without warning, Mr Munro appeared in the back shop where I was assembling an order.

"How are you getting on, Robert?" he asked while laying his attaché case down on a crate of cheese.

"Fine thank you, Mr Munro."

"I want a word with you, but let's wait until Mr Stewart is with us."

Gee, what's going on here? Have I done something wrong? I thought.

The boss must have seen Mr Munro arriving, as he came into the back shop.

"Right then, Robert. Mr Stewart tells me you're back here on a permanent basis. Is that correct?" he enquired, folding his arms and looking me straight in the eye.

"Yes."

"Why is that?"

"I wasn't learning anything in the TV job. I'm happier working here."

"What are your plans?"

The boss, wiping his hands on a cloth, came to join us.

"Well, I enjoy the work here and want to learn as much as possible."

"Do you want to be a manager some day?" he said with a little smile.

"Oh, I don't know about that."

"Well, we'd like to offer you an indenture."

"What does that mean, Mr Munro?"

"It means you'll have a contract with the company and be secure in your work here for the next three years. What do you think about that?"

"Sounds good. I'm hoping to start grocery evening classes in Dundee in August. Will I be allowed to do that?"

"Of course. We'd hope you would."

"Classes are on Monday and Tuesday evenings, but on Mondays I'll need to leave the shop at half-past five so that I can be home for tea and then get the train to Dundee."

"That's not a problem. Will you see to that, Mr Stewart?" he asked, turning towards the boss.

"Yes, yes," he promptly replied.

"Fine. Right, Robert. I'll bring that contract for you to sign the next time I visit."

"Thanks, Mr Munro."

It seemed like a progressive step for me, and I told mum that evening. She was really pleased.

"That's good. It shows the company likes your work."

Lying in bed that night, I pondered on the meaning of the word "contract". It seemed serious, but something I was comfortable with.

At the first opportunity I asked Jock.

"Have you got an apprentice contract?"

"No, no. Nothing like that. I'm in a safe, family-run quality business. No need for a contract!"

The *Dundee Courier and Advertiser* newspaper printed a page of evening classes available at the city's Commercial College. I went to Jock's house to discuss the matter.

"Are you still thinking of going to classes?"

"Oh yes, Robbie. What about you?"

"My area manager is hoping I'll go."

"That's good. Johnny along at Bradburns has said he'll be going too."

* * *

On an August evening Jock Brown, myself and Johnny Robb went by steam train to Dundee East railway station, then walked to the former Cowgate Primary School near the Wishart Arch to enrol in The Grocers' Institute Preliminary Certificate course. On the way home in our own compartment on the train, Jock triumphantly declared: "Here we are then, lads – the three grocery musketeers!"

A routine was established: rush home on a Monday for tea, then dash on my bike to the railway station when sometimes I was in such a rush that I'd have no time to lock my bike. Tuesday being half day was more relaxed, and Jock, Johnny and myself eventually developed a plan to go to Dundee for a walkabout. We were all interested in cars and toured around show rooms. Johnny was desperate to buy a motor scooter and gazed at Vespas and Lambrettas until we had to drag him away. It was also a chance to do some shopping, then more regularly go to a cinema. The Kinnaird, La Scala and Green's Playhouse were our haunts. It was at Green's where we went one Tuesday afternoon later in the year to watch Bill Haley and The Comets in 'Rock Around the Clock', and discovered it was true that lots of people got out of their seats to jive in the aisles. Our Tuesdays became a great routine, as we had a fish supper tea in the "Deep Sea" restaurant in Nethergate and then went on to our evening class. What was so good about the classes was that we could relate the theory to the practice. I could check on product information in the shop or ask the boss for answers.

The curriculum was set by the London-based Grocers' Institute and applied to students across the UK. Our subjects included product knowledge, accounts, business and commerce principles, window displays, and world geography. The pattern was now set. Increasing practical experience in the shop, with growing responsibilities and a winter of evening classes.

At long last I now felt the stuttering start to my working life was over, and the prospect of evening classes gave me focus and allowed me to chat with my pal Willie about our respective studies. He had started his building construction and technical theory classes at Dundee Technical College, and we had some interesting evenings learning from each other – although we each had homework to keep us busy. One evening a week at the cinema was the extent of our midweek outings, and meeting up with pals in Tommy Swan's café for a coffee or hot orange drink.

One Thursday evening we set off to the cinema, but the Regal had a lacklustre programme so we walked to the Pavilion. There we found no films showing, but the Newton Panbride church drama group were presenting a play which was about to commence in ten minutes. With little else to do in small town Carnoustie, we stepped inside. There – to my amazement – I found one of my former assistant Scout masters on the stage, and likewise two or three of my old Sunday School teachers. It was a humorous play, and they all seemed to be enjoying themselves greatly. Shortly afterwards I met my one-time Scout master in the street and said how much I had enjoyed the play. He encouraged me to join, saying there could be a small part in a play for me. I remember going along to my first meeting and wondering what my pals would think of me showing off on a stage. What I found was a group of enthusiastic people, some of whom I knew, and quickly found a rapport with them. Unknown to me at the time, this was to serve as another building block in my life. Everything seemed always to fall into place without any effort by myself. Meeting Harry Reid and joining the Cubs, meeting Jim and the adventures which followed at Westhaven – to say nothing of his offer of a message boy job – and then Mr Munro's encouragement to attend evening classes.

* * *

One Monday afternoon, Mr Munro was in the shop and asked me how I was getting on.

"Fine," I replied.

"Are you learning now? And your classes, how are they going?" he enquired in a serious tone.

"All okay, Mr Munro."

"Have you any questions?"

"None at all."

"Good. Did you put in this display?" Using his folded reading spectacles, he pointed to the fruit window. He meant 'had I dressed it?'

"No."

"Why not?" he asked, his eyebrows raised.

"I haven't been asked yet."

I'd been desperate for a while to make a window display, and I was keen to write the artistic price tickets in the style the company used. It was a remaining skill to pick up, and I wanted to do it before Jock. The boss did it all himself, and I understood why. It was his branch, and he would want to maximise sales so I was hesitant to ask him. But now that Mr Munro had asked me I felt better. When the boss was free from the counter, he approached us. Mr Munro said "Ian, this young man wants to try his hand at putting in a window. Can you give him a chance sometime?"

"Yes, of course."

The subject hadn't been raised by me, but Mr Munro gave the boss the impression that I had. Did the boss think I had complained or was critical of him, which had prompted Mr Munro to raise the subject? However, he seemed to accept Mr Munro's comments. Eventually Mr Stewart guided me step by step, and I gradually developed the skill of dressing the fruit window. He gave me old pieces of white cardboard on which to practise writing price tickets, and eventually my tickets were used. That was a big step, and I was secretly thrilled and felt that I was beginning to help the boss a lot more.

While we were waiting on the platform for the train one evening, Jock remarked: "I saw you putting in your fruit window today. Our windows are used for quality delicatessen products and wines and spirits. It's not about throwing apples and pears on trays."

He didn't say he'd dressed his window, but I didn't pursue it. His boss was the only one I ever saw do it. My gentle competition with Jock was still very much alive.

* * *

A strange coincidence happened around this time. I had gone to a dance at Barry Church hall, and the man at the doorway taking tickets was someone I recognised.

"You're Robert Murray, aren't you?" he said as I passed over my ticket.

Wondering what he was about to say, I warily confirmed that I was.

"I was with your uncle Jim when he was killed."

I had known my uncle died at El Alamein, but I was so shocked by the unexpected comment. Because there was a queue behind me, I had no chance to speak with the friendly man. I dearly wanted to ask how my uncle died and I wondered all evening whether I should approach him, but decided he may be upset if I asked him for details. He must have seen some terrible things. The next day I told mum and dad about the man, and they said they knew him.

"Yes, that would have been Alan Simpson. He's told us before that he was with Jim in North Africa," said dad.

"He's a lovely man, and was very badly injured with shrapnel," mum added.

"Has he ever told you how uncle Jim died?" I asked.

"No, we've never asked."

This surprised me, as a coloured picture of my uncle had hung on the landing wall at home for years and dad, quite emotional, always attended the War Memorial service. But strangely, no one in the house ever discussed the subject. It gave me the impression that it wasn't the correct thing to ask about such matters. I couldn't help thinking what a shame it was that uncle Jim had given his life and no one ever spoke about it.

The coincidence occurred when, a few days later, I spoke with mum about needing a suit to wear when singing in the church choir on Sunday evenings.

"I've never had a suit to wear to church, mum. I think I'll have to buy one."

"Wait a minute," she said, and disappeared to her bedroom.

"Here you are. Try this on for size," she suggested as she handed me a complete suit on a hanger.

"Where did that come from, mum?"

"It was your uncle Jim's, and it's been in my wardrobe since 1942."

Suddenly the stories I had heard many years before about Jim flooded back to me. How he had looked in to see me and mum prior to him sailing to Africa; the letter which was 'returned to sender' and had reported on my progress as a one year old; how he had been measured for a suit to wear on his return. Now I was being offered that suit, and I felt utterly unworthy of it because I hadn't even had the courage to ask Alan Simpson how Jim was killed.

"I don't think I can wear his suit, mum. Uncle Jim should have come home to wear it, and it's too sad," I said, becoming emotional.

"He would want you to wear it. It's too small for dad, and it's quality material so I'm not going to throw it out. It's been waiting here for you. Go, try it on."

As soon as I stepped into the trousers then felt the silky, smooth lining of the jacket, I felt the most amazing closeness to a man I'd never known. I couldn't get out of my mind the unfairness that Jim had planned a suit for himself and yet never wore it. I had been told he was twenty-one years old when he died and that he was of small stature, which was probably the main reason he was batman to Colonel Blair-Imrie. And yet the suit fitted me – sixteen on my next birthday – perfectly. I wore that suit with reverence for nearly two years until I outgrew it, and I constantly wished that I could have thanked my uncle – as well as for him to know it had seen good church service. I never plucked up the courage to speak with Alan Simpson about Jim, but I vowed I would someday go to pay homage to him at El Alamein – and I did, after I retired.

Dad always said he would like to visit Jim's grave, and I never found a way to take him. Sadly it was after he died that I discovered a trip arranged by the British Legion, and I made the journey – I felt, on behalf of the entire family past and present – and brought back video film of the Military Cemetery and Jim's resting place. That was a tearful moment for mum and the family.

* * *

Mr Stewart had rarely had a break, but one evening he said he was to be on holiday and that Cathie would be in charge for a week. Ah! Is that why Mr Munro wanted me to dress a window and write tickets? And why the boss showed me how to make a streaky?

"Are you going to be able to do everything I've shown you when I'm away?" he asked me as he counted the day's takings.

"Yes, I'll be alright."

The week he was away offered a huge opportunity. Cathie did all the paperwork and cashing up. I did the fruit window and the streaky, and she did the provisions window – helped by me. It was a brilliant week and, for me, a huge step forward.

CHAPTER 15

Evening Class Success, or "Throw Him Out of the Ring!"

Spring 1958

BY Spring 1957 I had been an apprentice for a year. The Grocers' Institute preliminary examination was held in April.

To my astonishment I was notified that I was the third best student in Scotland, and was invited to collect my certificate and prize in Edinburgh at the end of June. A family owner of a grocery business in Carnoustie, where Jock worked, came into the shop one day.

"Well done, Robbie! I'm told you've won a prize. I'm driving to Edinburgh to pick up the Institute's Master Grocer's award. Would you like to come with me?"

"That's great, thanks."

"So, you're nearly a greasy grocer after all," said the boss one morning as I was skinning a cheese. "I'll need to tell Munro about your success."

Jock Brown had heard about it from his boss.

"What's this I hear about you picking up a prize, Robbie?"

Not to boast, I said: "Could be your turn next year, Jock. You never know – there may be a special prize for quality wines and spirits."

Spring brought another surprise – although not entirely unexpected – for, after a winter of rehearsing on Friday evenings, I was ready to take to the stage in my first performance. My rapport with the dramatic club members was strong, and I couldn't wait to be first in the church hall for meetings. Duties I took upon myself were to switch on the gas fire and set out the chairs where we read and rehearsed our lines. Once we knew our lines, I would mark out the stage on the floor and position make-believe furniture and props.

The club performed each year in the Pavilion cinema, which was closed by the generous owner to allow us to perform our shows. I discovered how the 'sets' and 'flats' were prepared and – on my Tuesday afternoon off – I, along with my former Scout master (I now addressed him as John), loaded a borrowed open-top lorry to transport props and furniture to the stage door. We presented a three-act play for three evenings to near-capacity audiences, and in 1957 it was *The Happiest Days of Your Life*. I played the small part of Hopcroft Minor. The play was advertised in shop windows throughout the town using props and black and white still photographs, and I featured in one or two. I remember thinking how scary it was – what if I made a mess of my part and forgot my lines? But the support and advice I received was encouraging, and I found myself on the stage where – a year previously – I had seen my old Scout master. Now I was on stage with him. Nobody today believes me when I say that I couldn't speak to girls back then, or really to converse at all, but unknown to me at the time my drama experiences began to provide me with growing self-belief.

* * *

Autumn 1957 brought a new round of dramatic club readings, and with even more zeal I launched myself into reading the part of an ancient retainer in a three-act play entitled *Ghosts and Old Gold* to be put on as usual in the Pavilion cinema in Spring.

It was also time to enrol for the second year of studies. Success in this would mean I would become an Associate Member of the Grocer's Institute. Retail legal aspects, tea tasting and coffee roasting were added to the previous syllabus. Our Monday evening and Tuesday afternoon arrangement continued as before, and I remember we used one Tuesday afternoon to watch Elvis Presley in *Jailhouse Rock* at Green's Playhouse cinema. It was a time of change in the music world, and *Top of The Pops* was something I rushed home to see on our newly-acquired first rental television set. The shop closed at six o'clock and I usually missed the early part of the programme, but I still managed to keep my whistling up to date while working in the back shop.

It was about this time that new products emerged. A frozen food cabinet was delivered to the branch, and we were told to encourage sales. The brand labels were Bird's Eye and Findus, and the products were peas, fish fingers and ice cream. I overheard some customers remark that it was just a fad and would never catch on. Sales were meagre. Another innovative arrival was Tetley tea bags. Would blended tea in packets die out? Customers were wary of tea bags, and rightly so. I had learned at night classes that the tea in bags was what the trade called 'dust and fannings'. This was the residue after tea leaves were tossed about to dry in the sun in the country of origin. Being dust, it didn't need time to brew, so it became known as 'quick brew' or 'instant tea'. When I told Jock we were now stocking this new tea product, he replied: "You see, Robbie, my customers would never buy that rubbish." Secretly, I thought he was right.

Evening classes continued, and on Tuesdays Jock, Johnny and I enjoyed our afternoons at a picture house in Dundee followed by our favourite fish and chip tea. We were told one Monday evening that we were not to have a regular teaching evening the next night: it was going to be revision instead. We convinced ourselves that our notes were fine and – as Jock had said – "Who needs revision anyway?" So we decided during our chippie meal to give classes a miss and go instead to watch the professional wrestlers Jackie Pallo, Mick McManus and Bert Royal in action at the Caird Hall. I was amazed to see posh Jock off his seat and repeatedly screaming at the wrestlers. "Throw him out of the ring! He's a cheat!" he kept repeating.

Eventually I pulled him down into his seat.

"It's just quality acting, Jock."

It was quite entertaining, and the only time we missed a class. In due course, we all sat and passed our second year Institute exams and became Associates. It sounded very grand, but that was the way the Institute worked. It was a long-standing organisation dating back to the early 1900s.

* * *

Bill Campbell had been energetically and cleverly organising a bus most Saturday evenings to take a crowd of lads of around my age to dances. Favourite venues were Brechin, Kirriemuir and Forfar, and sometimes Arbroath. He seemed to have information about when dances were held in town halls, and so the word went around whenever a bus was arranged. It was a novel idea with a new scene and different girls, but I don't think the enthusiastic Bill attempted to make any money from the venture as we paid a minimal cost. One disadvantage was that it was not possible to walk a girl home because, with lack of local geography, it was never clear how far away a girl lived and – if the bus left on time – you could be stranded far from home. Another downside was that some lads would disappear and take that risk, and Bill delayed the bus for as long as possible which meant sitting around on a bus doing nothing. Sometimes Bill decided we had waited long enough!

Willie and I discussed the problem of the dances and began to think of buying motorbikes, but during the past year three of our friends had been killed in bike accidents.

"What's the answer, Willie?" I asked one day while we sat drinking hot jungle juice (mixed fruit) at Tommy Swan's popular café.

"My mum will go mad if I suggest this, but I think we need to be independent and get motorbikes," Willie replied, running his hands around his hot glass.

"With Roddy, Sandy and Bill now dead, I've got no hope of my mum saying yes. But we'll need to think of something clever."

It took some weeks of deliberation, but we finally came up with a solution.

"I've convinced my mum that I can do extra night class work with flexible travel times using a bike instead of waiting for buses," said Willie as we walked along the High Street.

"My mum's slowly coming around to the idea because dad may be doing more relief work soon, and once I pass my test I could take him to out-of-the-way signal boxes when there are no trains to take him,"

We agreed to keep up the pressure, and applied for provisional licences. A few other lads had bikes, so we could join up with them on bike runs and to dances. On my Tuesday afternoons in Dundee, I started looking at bikes in a showroom in the Overgate. Just to walk around the showroom with the smell of petrol and engines was enticing, and the urge to jump on a bike and go was over-powering. Against my mum's better judgement, and shortly after my seventeenth birthday, I bought for sixty-nine pounds a 350cc Triumph 3T bike, complete with an ex-army telescopic stand.

Willie bought himself a BSA 250cc motorbike which he used to travel to and from his evening classes, and we used the bikes on several occasions to attend dances and go for joyrides around the countryside. Until we had passed our road test we were legally not allowed a pillion passenger, but on rare occasions late at night we did. Bikes handled differently with a passenger, and Willie had a scare once. When failing to take a sharp bend, he and his luckless passenger ended up in a muddy turnip field. I had a lucky escape when I forgot to pull up the telescopic stand and consequently couldn't take a left-hand bend; being on the wrong side of the road, I came face-to-face with a car travelling towards me. We both braked and faced each other only three feet away, with the car driver looking distinctly horrified – probably mirroring myself.

We began to have a regular Sunday run on our bikes around country roads, and one of our early drives to Dundee was to see Billy Fury perform in a massive circus tent at Riverside Park. We felt our independent transport arrangements were paying off.

Willie and I had earned holiday time off, and we discussed our options for a motorbike tour.

"We could go to Glasgow and stay with my aunt and uncle," Willie suggested.

"That's not a bad idea. I have an aunt and uncle in Greenock. We could go there too."

A grand tour was arranged, and we travelled along the banks of Loch Lomond then along the Ayrshire coast – with added boat trips on Clyde steamers. Sadly, this was to be our first and last motorbike touring holiday, as Willie – for some reason unknown to me – made a dramatic decision, despite excellent results at college, to leave his joinery apprenticeship and join the Royal Navy. Clearly Willie had problems of some sort which he never discussed, and it was an unsettling time for me as I missed his company.

When I later passed my test, I was able to drive dad to his out-of-the-way signal boxes and mum relaxed her worries.

Once, alone and on a cold and wet night, I drove to Kirriemuir for a dance in the Town Hall there. Wearing my dad's black heavy British Rail great coat, my 'Biggles goggles' and my crash helmet (reminiscent of a decapitated egg top), I knew I was no James Dean. Alas, I arrived soaked to the skin and spent the whole evening drying off beside a radiator. No girl to dance with that night. I sat my motorbike driving test in Arbroath and, having driven around streets in figures-of-eight several times and doing an emergency stop when the instructor jumped out from behind a parked car, I surprisingly passed. My motorcycling days ended literally with a crash when a car driver came around a bend on the wrong side of the road and knocked me off my bike. After a night in Dundee Royal Infirmary, with luckily only a broken wrist, I decided I must get myself a car. After much anguish, mum was at last comfortable with my sensible decision.

* * *

In August 1958 we enrolled for the next year of our course – the 'Membership' stage. Studies would be more advanced, including accounts, commercial law, and more product knowledge. Our teacher – Mr Fred Leitch, a plump man who always wore an immaculate three-piece suit – had been in Burma during WW2. His grocery knowledge was extensive. He had also been a sales representative, and knew many of the top Scottish manufacturers. He regaled us with interesting tales of Burma and of the successes of Gordon Baxter, owner of Baxter's Soups, along with other well-known Scottish entrepreneurs.

Mr Leitch informed us that St Michael was the patron saint of soldiers, doctors, mariners and grocers. The Worshipful Company of Grocers was established in London in the year 1345, originally for 'grossers' and 'mercers'. He told us the Grocers' Institute was modelled on that medieval organisation, and set up mainly as an educational body. He advised us the Institute operated a home study scheme whereby we could pay a fee and be supplied with course notes for each subject – and, where appropriate, product samples. I thought this was a good idea, and decided to take part. Samples of each product were sent to me in a small tin box about the size of a sardine can, and up to ten boxes packed into a custom built cardboard box. Each pack contained samples of the grades and characteristics of each product. I found the information supplemented my class notes, and judged the cost would be good value.

Using the samples, I was better informed about various products. They included:

Tea: I still remember some of the names. Green, Lapsang Souchong, Darjeeling, Gunpowder, Pekoe, Orange Pekoe, Broken Orange Pekoe, Dust and Fannings. There were teas from India, East Africa, and China.

Rice: For example; Patna, American, Japanese, Sumatra, with special attention to hard and soft grain varieties.

Coffee: We learned that fundamentally there are only two types in the world; Robusta and Arabica. Each type had varying characteristics depending upon countries of origin, such as Kenya, Colombia, and Brazil.

Some distinctions were almost negligible, but I overcame the problem by asking mum to move the tins around, hide the label, then ask me to identify. We had some great laughs when I got things wrong, and she learned along with me.

When I was studying during winter evenings, mum made life more comfortable for me. Very scarily she would bring a shovel of burning coal upstairs to my bedroom and place the 'instant fire' in my fireplace. She was always very supportive.

During that same winter, and with the success of *Ghosts and Old Gold* behind us, the drama club was rehearsing for a performance in the Beach Hall in Spring 1959 of *Sailor Beware*. I had been cast in my biggest role so far as the supporting character of Carnoustie Bly, the dour Scottish shipmate of Albert who was to be played by Scout master John.

Willie, after basic training, came home on leave and we caught up with each other. He told me about his exciting trips to London, local dances (without motorbikes), free issues of 'Blue Liner' cigarettes, and daily rations of rum – all in addition to the training he was now receiving as an electrical engineering naval student.

During that leave, Willie constantly complained of a serious itch on his legs. I encouraged him to go to a doctor, but he said he would wait until he went back to Lee-on-Solent.

"Too many free rum rations, Willie," I teased.

"Naw; I'm just itching to sail around the world," Willie quipped.

CHAPTER 16

London, or
"Miss Black! Your Umbrella!"

Spring 1959

"IT'S a great bargain, Robbie," said Tom, a grocer with the Co-op Society in the town. He was about a year older than me, and I met him occasionally around town when we often chatted about the grocery trade – but more especially about cars and motorbikes.

We were in Glamis, because we had read of a Wolseley 14 car for sale at £27. The price included many spare parts. We were driven there by a pal, and Tom – who had passed his car driving test – came with me to drive the Wolseley back home should I decide to buy it.

I'd had my dim experiences with Bill Campbell's bus in-itiative and my wet nights in Kirriemuir Town Hall, and I thought a car would be the answer. It was a large car, but I took the chance because I knew some lads who would share the cost of trips to dances. Tom kindly offered to teach me how to drive (unknown by his boss) on the Co-op milk van on the grassy avenue between summer huts at Buckiehillocks. He also sat with me while we travelled to venues. It proved to be a popular mode of transport for five or six of us (no seat belts in those days) on a Saturday evening or for Sunday trips. One day I spotted a problem with the wheels and decided to sell it, which I did for £32 – a profit! Tom was called up to do National Service and I hastened on with my driving tuition, finally passing my driving test in Arbroath.

* * *

One dreary, wet Saturday afternoon, I had a more searching test. The shop was packed, and all staff – including myself – were serving. Dripping raincoats created pools of water where customers queued. It was the practice, having completed a sale, to call out 'next please'. This I did, and stepping out from behind a very large gentleman was my next customer. A small lady, almost hidden beneath a large drooping hat. No, it couldn't be... but yes, it was! Miss Black! The formidable Miss Black, the Post Office lady who told me off for not counting my coins!

Looking quite flustered, she approached me and stood opposite the part of the counter I occupied.

Did she recognise me? Did it matter? I had never previously seen her in the shop.

"Hello," I said.

"Oh dear me, I've lost my list," she said in her deep voice.

Recalling her tough attitude towards me, I immediately faced an overpowering question: how do I handle her? I made an instant decision. She's my customer, and I must treat her as I would all the others.

She continued to rustle through all her pockets, and then in desperation said: "Oh well, I'll try from memory. Two pounds of sugar."

No "please" or "thank you".

"A plain loaf."

Still searching, she added: "A quarter of tea. That one – the sixpence one," she said, pointing to the tea shelf. Then: "A pound of carrots."

I went to the back shop, weighed them, then washed my hands. On my return: "A quarter of boiled shoulder." Then: "Three and a half pounds of potatoes."

Off to the back shop once more, then wash my hands again. During my brief absence, she had apparently found her list.

"Oh, no – it's six ounces of boiled shoulder."

Silently humming the same tune as the boss while serving Mrs Rigg, I continued to deal with Miss Black's needs. In retrospect, I can't imagine what my smile must have looked like.

"Anything else today, now?"

"No, that'll be all. Oh, no – give me six eggs."

Fashioning a papier maché tray, I tied the parcel with string. I then totalled the amount, received her money, and gave change.

"Can I help you to pack these, now?"

"No, I can do that."

While passing over her groceries, she struggled with her wet bag and raincoat and accidentally dropped the eggs. It looked like they had survived, but she insisted I check. One was cracked, so I replaced it and went through the process again.

Her bag packed, she suddenly called out: "Oh, no – I need a big packet of Persil."

That was kept in the back shop, so I dealt with it, received payment, and she was at long last ready to go.

"Thank you very much, Miss Black."

With no "sorry" or any blushes, she muttered in a half-hearted way: "Thank you."

As she walked away, I noticed her umbrella hooked over the rail where she had stood in such disarray.

"Miss Black! Your umbrella!"

She turned around. "Oh, thanks."

Don't lose your list next time was a phrase I held under my breath. It seemed to match her command: "Count your coins next time." I also couldn't help seeing the funny side of her umbrella situation being a bit like her calling to me about my buttons. "Go, go, greasy grocer go" I said to myself, but at the same time my respect for her grew and I now saw her as a highly-trained professional Post Office clerk.

Miss Black did me a great favour; she wouldn't have been aware but, for me, it was a huge lesson about dealing with customers. They were all the same, no matter.

* * *

The reason the dramatic club play *Sailor Beware* was performed in the Beach Hall was because the club had been informed that the Institute of Sanitary Inspectors was to hold its annual conference in the nearby Bruce Hotel in the town. Our club decided, as a mark of hospitality, to admit them free of charge. This helped to swell our audience numbers, and the show went off without a hitch – except when my wee sister Jean called out from the audience: "That's my daddy's shoe!" when she saw Carnoustie Bly (aka Robbie) flicking cigarette ash into my dad's borrowed black shoe while Albert and Carnoustie were chatting in bed.

* * *

"There's a letter here for you with an English post mark," said mum one day when I arrived home for lunch.

"Great! That'll be from Willie," I said, for I received regular updates of his escapades in his sailor's uniform and couldn't wait for his latest instalment.

I was dismayed to read that my friend had written from his hospital bed to say he had been admitted with a head injury when, working in the engine room of a vessel, a hammer had fallen on him. There was no other news, and all I could do was to write a reply and send it to his normal address.

"Do you think it's serious?" mum asked when I told her.

"I don't know, mum. But it must have been bad if he ended up in hospital for a few days."

* * *

Busy days at the counter, when everyone was serving, continued. Behind the counter, space to work was limited, and inevitably pieces of bacon, fat or preserving jelly fell onto the wooden floor. On rainy days, the problem was exacerbated by wet shoes. At the end of such a day I had to scrape the sticky build-up with a garden hoe. I took it upon myself to go to the local joiner's yard for a box of sawdust.

"The wee greasy grocer's learning about the grease," the boss chanted. "Go, go, greasy grocer go!"

On those non-stop days, another problem manifested itself. Being on my feet all day, I developed a 'flat' foot: I discovered that I couldn't put my right heel down when I walked. The arch of my foot seemed to have collapsed and couldn't support me, and I walked with a 'floppy' foot which made a flapping noise as I moved about.

"What's wrong with your foot, Robert?" the boss asked me.

"I don't know – it's just something that's started. I'll need to see the doctor about it."

"Och, it'll be alright. It'll come and go. It's called Grocer's Foot."

"Do you think I'll have two flat feet someday?"

"You never know."

Was the boss teasing me? It was then I realised that the boss did walk with 'funny' feet. After my short life as a grocer, I couldn't believe that I had already developed a body fault.

"It's a fallen arch," mum said when I told her about my problem. "It'll get better when you're stronger."

Mum was right again – it did.

My foot problem didn't deter me from dancing, and it seemed there were many options. The Saturday favourite was the Marine Ballroom in Arbroath, where my friends and I enjoyed dancing to a live band. It was very well managed, with bouncers (although we didn't call them that in those days) at the door who turned boys away if they were badly dressed, behaving badly through alcohol, or had been previously banned for poor conduct. Another must were the dances held weekly in the Beach Hall, Carnoustie, where we danced to records so that it was all completely up to date with the latest hits. The lights were dimmed, and the sparkling revolving glass ball created special effects which added to the atmosphere of a slow dance with a girl to the sound of the Everly Brothers singing 'All I Have to Do is Dream" or Perry Como performing 'Magic Moments'.

I had what might be termed teenaged flights of fantasy, when I dreamed all week about dancing with Rosemary every Wednesday evening. But her mum was a member of the Dramatic Club and – as I had learned Rosie was around four years younger than me – I thought it best not to cause a problem. Small town syndrome strikes again!

* * *

The Institute's examination for the year was to be in two parts. A written test for course work would be held in Dundee, with practical skills such as product identification, tea tasting and coffee roasting tested in London. Success in the written part would trigger the trip to London.

We met in the college to be informed of results by Mr Leitch. From a class of twelve students, two of us – Ronnie, a bright go-getter from Fife, and myself – booked the adventurous journey to London for the second part. We were joined by canny Dundonian Jimmy – who, like us, had paid for a week's bed and breakfast in advance, but sadly failed the written test. The three of us decided to treat it as a tourist trip, with some tests thrown in for Ronnie and me.

"How are we going to get to London then?" said Jimmy, who – despite his disappointment – was eager to set up plans.

"A sleeper on the train would be far too costly," Ronnie observed.

"I've spoken with my dad, and he says there will be many spaces in the normal coaches," I suggested.

"Well, that's fine," responded Ronnie. "But what are we going to eat?"

"Why don't we just bring sandwiches and bottles of lemonade?" said Jimmy.

"That's the answer," I said. "And I'll bring cards."

The tests were to be held in an historic trading hall hired by the Institute in Eastcheap, on a Thursday, so our B&B booking for seven nights from the prior Tuesday meant we would travel by rail on Monday. This plan would give us two days before the exam, and four days afterwards.

We gathered with our suitcases and extra bags of food and drink, and occupied a dusty-smelling six-seat compartment in a corridor coach complete with toilets. The train, which was the Aberdeen-London overnight express, was one I'd seen often pass Admiral Street, Westhaven. We departed Dundee Tay Bridge Station at around seven o'clock in the evening. The three of us played cards all the way to Edinburgh, by which time Ronnie was the first to admit: "Do we have to keep playing like this all night?"

The card idea dimmed after we left Edinburgh and, after a spot of reading, we were able to put the armrests up and lie along on the long bench seat.

"It's alright, boys – there's nobody in the next compartment. I'll spread out there," called Jimmy as he opened the sliding door of our own compartment.

It was a long night, and the excitement of the trip didn't allow for any quality sleep.

Emerging from King's Cross railway station into the warm London sunlight at six o'clock in the morning was a relief, and we soon forgot our uncomfortable night.

"I'm famishing!" gasped Jimmy.

"You're not the only one!" Ronnie and I said in almost perfect unison.

A nearby café was the answer, where we made quick work of our plates of bacon, egg and beans. Food revived our energies, and all was well until the waitress refused to accept a Scottish £1 note offered by Ronnie.

"I've heard about this," moaned Jimmy. "Don't tell me we're going to have this bother wherever we go."

Ronnie produced a wad of notes, which probably didn't help the situation, and it was touch and go until he produced his cheque book showing the Royal Bank of Scotland logo which matched the note. Well done, Ronnie.

Impressions of London so far? Warm sun, tasty bacon and eggs, strange voices, and trouble with our money.

I'd passed through London with mum and dad nearly four years previously, and had briefly been on the Underground. It was enough for me to know about east bounds and north bounds. With the help of railway staff and what we thought were odd accents, we arrived at our bed and breakfast lodgings.

* * *

For a while, we forgot our impending tests and enjoyed the London scene. Mr Leitch had guided us on things to do and see. We got the hang of the Underground and darted about all over the place, visiting Trafalgar Square, Pudding Lane and St Paul's Cathedral amongst other well-known attractions.

Back in Fife, Ronnie had been told about a pub in Putney called 'Dirty Dick's' and had decided that he wanted to visit it. It seemed a luxury trip on even more tube trains, but we located it and decided to cool off with a beer. It was a busy, noisy pub by the River Thames, and the interior was decorated with dried rats, mice, cat skeletons and mousetraps. The place smelled, with a mixture of stale ale, tobacco smoke and spicy food in the air. I didn't like the look of it at all.

"Three half pints of beer, please," requested Jimmy.

"What kind o' beer di' ya want, mate?"

Jimmy enquired: "What kind have you got?" He then received an unintelligible reply which reeled off many meaningless names – presumably beers.

The busy bartender didn't have time to explain things to three foreigners, so he said: "I'll give you some bitter."

We were standing beside Jimmy, but didn't have time to express a view to him before he over zealously said: "Okay, that'll be fine." His Scottish accent seemed all out of place, even for Ronnie and me.

Despite the strange surroundings, we were excited to be standing in a London pub on the banks of the Thames – all agog at the weird internal décor. But the joy turned to dismay when we tasted the beer.

"That's no beer," Ronnie blurted.

"No, it's rubbish," I said.

"What do you think Jimmy?" Ronnie asked him.

Jimmy, in trying to defend his purchase, replied: "Aye, it's no' quite as good as the stuff I get in Dundee."

"Oh, come on, Jimmy!" insisted Ronnie. "It's disgusting!"

Well, we'd seen Dirty Dick's and the artificial (I think!) rats and cats, so we headed back for the Underground station – leaving three almost-full half-pints of bitter.

Once on the tube, Jimmy having had time to collect his thoughts, said: "Sorry lads, that was my fault. I thought the barman had told me 'I'll give you something better'."

"No, he definitely said 'bitter'," Ronnie noted, and I added: "A bitter lesson for us all."

I had another expensive lesson the next day. Feeling the heat and the tiredness of moving about the London streets, I saw a little shop selling bottles of Coca Cola. I ordered a bottle of coke and, as an impulse buy, asked for a slice of chocolate cake.

Offering a pound note, because I wanted change, the foreign assistant said: "Seven and six, please." As she unashamedly held up my pound note, then flicked it between her thumb and middle-finger, I was stunned. A bottle of Coke in Carnoustie was ninepence, and a slice of cake around a shilling. It seemed like a good idea at the time.

"I'm throwing away my money," I said dispiritedly. "I'll need to watch my budget, lads."

Fred Leitch hadn't mentioned visiting Downing Street, but believing we had to pack in as much sight-seeing as possible we planned to visit. I vividly recall how we walked along a deserted Downing Street to Number 10 at midnight, and spoke to the 'Bobby' on duty who was standing – stock-still, like an army guardsman – at the front door. I was quite certain he wouldn't want to be troubled by three Scots lads creating a nuisance.

"How long do you have to stand like that?" asked Ronnie, always the friendly Fifer.

No reply from the statue-like figure.

"Come on, boys" I said. "We'll be arrested for causing trouble."

"Would you like a sweetie?" asked the ever-generous Jimmy in his jaunty style.

Then the motionless guardian at the door spoke.

"No thanks. You fellas down from the North, then?

"Eh, we're frae Dundee, ken?" said Jimmy, putting on an over-emphasised Dundee accent.

"I thought I detected a Dundee voice there. Enjoyin' yourselves in the smoke, then?"

This person's real, and even speaks!

"Aye, we're here on holiday for a week," I said. "Do you know Dundee, then?"

"Of course. I grew up in Lochee."

This London Bobby was immediately transformed into one of us – a Scotsman!

"How long do have to stand here?" asked a more confident Ronnie.

"Until six."

"How do you manage to stand here all night like this?" Ronnie enquired politely.

"This helps a bit," said the now-relaxed Scotsman as he removed his helmet to reveal a small transistor radio fixed inside, which we could hear. It was the Platters, singing 'Smoke Gets in Your Eyes'.

We all laughed.

"On your way then, boys. Behave yourselves, and enjoy your holiday."

We walked back to get a tube to our digs.

"Would you believe that?" said Jimmy wonderingly. "Four Scots havin' a blether at the door o' Number 10!"

The glamorous side-show of London came to an end, and we had to turn up for our serious examinations on Thursday morning at eleven o'clock as required. Ronnie and I had planned our journey, and found our way to the exam venue in time. The building was quite intimidating from the outside, but once inside it was even more impressive. The structure was similar to that of a church, with great wooden roof beams and plastered walls with plaques and stone tablets attached. It looked ancient, but not medieval as I'd expected. The busy chatter and noises seemed to echo around the vast area of the hall. There was a buzz of activity with what appeared to be fellow students. There were many dozens of them, who seemed confidently to know exactly what do. It looked daunting, and I began to wonder if I really wanted to be there. We registered and found that students had been asked to book in at separate times – presumably to spread activity across the day. Ronnie and I found ourselves in separate groups. The system required that I would move from point to point and be tested on each aspect. I immediately sensed my vulnerability in the mass of people and general clamour.

Product identification was first: merely a selection of cereals and pulses such as peas, beans, rices, sago, tapioca, farina. Nothing new there! Then tea tasting. Initially I had to examine a few dry samples which were relatively easy to identify as they were of distinct, extreme types. Tasting was more straightforward than I anticipated, for the same reason. It was coffee roasting that I envisaged could be the trickiest test. However, I found the set up and procedure was as Mr Leitch had instructed, and that all went smoothly. The window display test consisted of making a symmetrical display using box-

es of product such as cans and packets. The entire test procedure was over before I knew it. It was all conducted in friendly fashion, and I sensed a genuine welcome extended to me as
a Scot.

Ronnie and I met up and reviewed our respective experiences. We concluded that the tests were easy. Did we really
need to go to London for them? I remember thinking that in
far-off days it was perhaps more a ritual of being accepted into
the olde-worlde Grocers' fraternity. Was it possibly more a
question of being accepted into the Honourable Body, and the
trip to London was a personal assessment as much as the skills
tests?

With the Grocers' Institute experience behind us, we
could now fully relax. Both Ronnie and I felt we had passed,
so it was time to return to our tourist agenda. Friday was
spent at Madame Tussaud's and then with walkabouts.

Mr Leitch hadn't suggested visiting Joe Loss and his
regular dance band, but I'd seen the band leader and his orchestra in a packed dance hall on lunchtime Saturday TV and
thought it would be a pleasant way to spend Saturday evening. We set off and joined a very long queue. Once inside the
famous Hammersmith Palais ballroom, and with Joe and his
famous orchestra only a few feet away, I glided along doing
my slow, slow, quick, quick, slow with a London lassie in my
arms. I imagined I had hit the big time!

One last daring adventure remained. Ronnie wanted to
see Hampton Court, and suggested we hire a car and have a
drive out there on Sunday. Our time in London was fast coming to an end, and this seemed a novel idea. We all went to a
car hire office. Ronnie was keen to do the driving, and we
knew he had only a provisional licence when he was asked if
he had full driving licence. Jimmy and I were astounded to

hear him report that yes, he did, but accidentally he'd left his licence certificate at home. The office clerk accepted his statement, and Ronnie signed to hire a very large Ford Zephyr.

To say it was nerve-wracking to drive through London and to Hampton Court was a gross understatement, but with the inexperienced Ronnie it was doubly so. Crunching gears, getting in the wrong lanes and swerving round corners became commonplace, and I truly thought danger was ahead. Ronnie's devil-may-care attitude overcame the reality. Driving the wrong way along a dual carriageway was the final straw for me and Jimmy. We screamed our heads off, and a subdued Ronnie miraculously drove the Ford back to base in one piece. I shudder to think how costly it could have been for Ronnie or his family if he'd killed anyone.

Not surprisingly, I can't remember anything about Hampton Court. I'm not sure to this day if we ever got there.

Confirmation of success was sent directly to my home address on elaborate Grocers' Institute letter-headed notepaper. All the homework had paid off. We had both passed and became Members of the Grocers' Institute. The next level was to study in order to become Master Members. Neither Ronnie nor myself ever did that. He was a son of a family grocery business and a key part of the firm, and felt he didn't need to do any more studying. For myself, I didn't think it was necessary for me given that I was working in a multiple grocery organisation.

Returning to my work in Carnoustie, and with the excitement of London and success behind me, I sat down one evening and pondered: *Where do I go from here?*

CHAPTER 17

Standing In For the Boss, or "How Would You Like to Manage a Branch?"

Spring 1960

S ALES of new products such as tea bags and frozen foods were almost non-existent, but business generally grew. It became difficult to meet the added demands at the counter.

"It's a serious day when I see customers walking out of the queue," the boss bemoaned as he came rushing through the back shop while I weighed potatoes on the scales. "Must get permission from Munro to take on extra staff," he added with urgency.

It wasn't difficult to understand that losing business in such a way was unacceptable. As a result, two additional assistants were engaged: one full-time, and another part-timer. I also felt the pressure at very busy times, but my work continued more or less the same.

In his place, the boss delegated to me a new and distinctly unhappy task which was to visit customers and collect debt. A ghastly chore, and initially I felt I couldn't do it because some unfortunate people – through no fault of their own – struggled financially. Deep down, I knew I couldn't refuse to carry out work I was asked to do.

Once I was sent to the home of Brian, a former classmate. That was more difficult than usual, and probably very embarrassing for him when he answered the door. I liked Brian, and I felt bad about calling at his house. My worst thought was that Brian may never speak to me again. My hesitant feeling about the visit wasn't helped by the fact that I was not given any guidance on what to say or how to speak to the customer. I just had to get on with it, and my stomach was churning as I cycled my way along the street while trying to rehearse my words. All too soon I was at the door.

"Hello Brian," I said, trying to sound upbeat.

"Oh hello, Robbie!" he replied with a smile breaking on his pasty white face.

"Is your mum in, Brian?" I asked with a more serious tone.

He called for his mum, who came immediately to the door. She had a strained expression when she first appeared and, on seeing me, became quite agitated and dropped a rubber glove which she was nervously trying to remove from her hand.

"Hello. It's about the money you're due. The boss asked me to say I had to collect what you owe for last month," I managed to say somehow, while forcing myself to make eye contact with her.

My pal may have overheard my words so, for his sake, I avoided the word 'debt'.

"Oh, is it due? Tell Mr Stewart I'll be along to the shop tomorrow," Brian's mum said in a matter-of-fact way.

"Alright, I will," I said without question.

I instantly made up my mind that this was an acceptable response and, as I walked away from the door and before it closed, I overheard Brian.

"Mum! You promised never again!" he said in anguish.

Another piece of confidential information.

As I cycled back to the shop, I couldn't help feeling so cruel. Why should a young person like me wield such power over the mother of a friend of mine? His mum was probably an excellent mother and housewife, but was merely trying to make ends meet. That was bad enough, but I could only imagine the damage my visit must have done to Brian's confidence and wellbeing.

One evening, while I was walking through the front shop on my way home, the boss looked up and spoke. "Right then, Robert. You've heard me say I'm on holiday soon," the boss remarked as he counted the cash takings for the day.

"Oh yes – you go next month, don't you?" I said, half guessing.

"That's right. And you're getting the keys!" the boss declared in a pragmatic tone.

"Keys? What keys?" I asked him with curiosity.

"The shop keys, of course," he replied casually.

"I didn't know we had spare keys," I said.

"We don't. You're going to be in charge," he announced calmly.

"What?" I almost shouted.

"Yes. I've spoken with Munro, and he suggested it," he pronounced, as though to terminate the discussion.

"Jings. There's still a lot I don't know," I pointed out defensively.

"Not much; just cashing up, paperwork and wages," he said as if it was almost trivial.

"Not much!" I repeated in a helpless sort of voice.

"I'll show you before I go. I'll need to tell Munro. Are you going to do it?" he almost demanded.

"Yes. Well," I took a deep breath. "Okay then." Immediately I was aware that I'd made a serious decision which I couldn't now reverse.

"Good. I'll be thinking about you when I'm fishing!" He said humorously.

The question staggered me, and I was nervous at the prospect. I didn't know whether to jump with joy or to seriously think of avoiding such a huge, testing prospect.

As I cycled home, my nerves turned to excitement at the thought of telling mum.

"You're a bit late tonight, Robert. Are you alright?" mum enquired as she was tidying up in the kitchen.

"Yes, everything's fine. But the boss wanted to speak with me," I said, trying to be calm.

"Oh, was there a problem?" mum asked with a note of alarm.

"No, quite the opposite. You'll never guess what's happened, mum."

"Oh! Something good I hope?" she smiled.

"Yes. Remember I told you the boss is going on holiday soon? Well, he's asked me to manage the shop for a week."

"That's good news. But are you worried about that?" mum said as she wrung out a dishcloth in the sink.

"I think I can do it, but I hope nothing goes wrong. The boss is going to show me the paperwork I need to do when he's away," I explained.

"Well, he wouldn't ask if he didn't think you could do it. That's a good step forward for you," she said reassuringly.

"Seems so, but I'll have to see how it all goes."

* * *

The boss taught me how to cash up, deal with the till float, prepare bank money, and check invoices against delivery notes. He briefed me on window displays, what stock to order, and how to deal with price changes. He also told me which sales representatives were likely to call in to the shop. This, I thought, could be a problem because reps – as they were called – worked for major suppliers, and sometimes had to stand patiently waiting in the shop until the boss (now me!) was free to place an order. What was more amazing: I was shown how to prepare staff wages. Their earnings were no longer secret. Soon I would be handing over pay packets to the ladies who were my seniors and long-time trainers. This prospect gave me a mix of emotions. Was it right for a young boy like me to hand out pay packets to the full-time staff, and especially to Cathie who was a long-serving employee? Yet for me, it would be a huge boost to my confidence. It never occurred to me that I would see myself as the boss.

At the end of each day during that momentous week, mum asked me the same questions: "How are things going? Are you managing everything?"

"So far all fine, mum," was my daily reply, although I had some worrying times.

I didn't tell her about the most daring moment in my grocery life. It was something I least expected, and it shook me to the core to deal with it. The boss had left a note with me of what fruit and vegetables to order with the Dundee wholesaler's salesman on Monday morning. The delivery arrived late on Monday afternoon. All the goods – including apples, pears, potatoes and carrots – arrived as required, and were deposited routinely on the floor of the back shop. But as I was checking the count, I noticed through the net bag of one of the two twenty-eight pound bags of carrots that it appeared to contain rotten items. It was not unusual to find one or two bad carrots in any one bag, but this looked worse. The driver handed me the delivery note to sign.

"I can't sign that until I have a look at the carrots," I said, summoning up courage from somewhere. I'd never had any discord in my grocery life until this moment, and I was aware of the impact of my blunt refusal. Would the wholesaler report me to my boss, or perhaps Mr Munro? Would Cathie and the staff think I was trying to be too big for my greasy shoes? Was I wrong just because I was nervous?

"They look okay to me" the driver remarked in an argumentative tone.

"Well I'll need to have a look," I said in a quavering voice while my head began to swim with fear as I ignored his reply.

I took a knife and opened the bag, and immediately found several rotten carrots.

"I'm going to have to tip them out to check," I explained, while the driver let out a long, obvious sigh of displeasure.

It was clear that too many were unacceptable.

"I'm sorry – what's your name?" I enquired politely.

"Davy," he grunted.

"Well I'm sorry, Davy. You'll have to take them back. I'll sign and note one bag returned unfit, but please tell your boss I must have another bag by Wednesday."

I helped Davy repack the net, and he put the altered delivery note in his dungaree pocket and went back to his lorry with the carrots.

It was then I realised that if the wholesaler wanted to be difficult with me, he may say he can't deliver any more carrots on Wednesday and the result would be lost sales and tough questions from the boss about how bad the carrots had actually been. My heart was still pumping when I told Cathie what had happened once she had returned from the counter.

"I'm sure you'll get more carrots on Wednesday, but if not you will have to phone another wholesaler. I'd phone the wholesaler now and report what's happened."

That was good advice, which I immediately took. I felt a lot better once I'd explained the situation and received a promise that another bag would be delivered on Wednesday.

I didn't tell mum that evening, but worried about what possible consequences might arise. I consoled myself that Cathie had not disagreed with my action, and that the wholesaler had made a promise to send another bag. Nevertheless, had I made an enemy of the driver who might be difficult with me in future? The answer came on Wednesday when Davy appeared with a bag of carrots.

"Here's your replacement bag, chief. Just sign the original delivery note, please," he asked courteously.

"Thanks, Davy," I said quietly, accepting his chief reference.

All was well, and I was merely left thinking *was it a try on?* Had the salesman admitted to Davy that the carrots were in fact substandard, and the young upstart laddie in Carnoustie was right?

The boss had told me I would receive a delivery of Crawford's biscuits sometime later in the week. On Wednesday, after the safe arrival of the carrots, I was feeling confident enough to explain to David the message boy that I needed the empty biscuit tins brought to the back door in readiness for the delivery.

"Just check and sort out all the tins up in the loft, and make sure all the Crawford's are stacked ready for pick-up. While you're up there, David, check the mice situation."

Nothing untoward happened, except on Friday when I had to deal with a big dog which came behind the provisions counter and grabbed a two inch-thick round of ox tongue and ran away. I had to chase the dog along the pavement, but it managed to get away. What would I have done with the meat anyway?

* * *

The last part I played in a dramatic club show was as Buttons in *Cinderella* during Christmas 1959. To attend rehearsals and put on a play on Christmas and Boxing Day was adventurous in the extreme, but somehow everything went well. Now it was Spring 1960, and I would be twenty in October. I had less time to attend rehearsals, but I looked back and couldn't believe the variety of parts I'd played. Part of me knew that some people would think I was a show-off, but deep down I knew this wasn't true – quite the opposite, in fact.

What I had found – again by luck – was a way of developing my self-confidence, and since that time I have always felt that some professional actors probably suffered in similar ways.

The event I didn't look forward to was handing over pay packets to staff at the close of business on Saturday evening. I knew I had to act fast by counting the takings and calculating each wage using the printed page which had been sent from head office showing National Insurance deductions. Once complete, all I had to do was put the appropriate money in the correct brown envelope. I started with Cathie's pay, and worked my way through each one. The problem in my mind was that I had to count the cash and do my paperwork on the marble part of the counter beside the till while all the staff were walking around me doing their end of day cleaning up.

I counted the contents of each pay packet and went over my calculations twice, but my heart was thumping and the more I hurried the more coins dropped from my hands as I put money in envelopes. My acute worry was that the staff probably saw my every move and were no doubt wondering if they were to get the correct pay. The worst mistake was to give someone another person's wages. I double checked all that, too. I wanted to avoid a queue waiting in a line for me to finish my work.

"Is everything alright there, Robert ?" said Cathie supportively.

"Yes, fine thanks, Cathie," I said, praying that it was.

I'd seen how the boss gave out the pay, but I couldn't remember in which order.

Did it matter?

With some luck, I finished my double-checks and wrote names on packets before staff had finished tidying. I put the packets in a sequence, with Cathie first and David last, then went to each in turn. While uttering a silent prayer all was well, I approached Cathie and handed over her pay.

"There you are, Cathie. Thanks for your help this week," I said, while thinking this could be my biggest ever blunder.

"Thanks," she replied, before teasingly adding: "No problem, so long as I've not got David's pay!"

I said thanks to each member of staff as I handed over their pay, then I noticed everyone subsequently found a reason to go to the back store or into some quiet place. I knew they were, quite rightly, making sure I'd given them the correct wages – and I didn't blame them!

No-one came with to me with a query, and they all seemed quite happy. Phew!

During every testing day, I nervously did all I had been briefed to do. One thing I had to make sure was that I didn't hide myself away in the office or elsewhere, and thus did not take my share of work at the counter. Teamwork had continued without interference by me, and handing over pay seemed an anti-climax.

I looked forward to mum's Saturday evening question, which came as predicted.

"It was great, mum. Everybody did their normal jobs all week."

"I'm sure Mr Stewart will be pleased," mum said encouragingly.

I did tell mum about the dog and the carrots, and my fears about the wages.

When the boss returned, I had to brief him on events. I told him about the carrots, which was my biggest worry.

"I'll have a word with the salesman," he said thought-fully. Then I told him the story about the dog, which was important to me because it represented loss.

"It would have to be the most expensive meat," the boss observed in an understanding way. "We'll just have to make up the loss somehow. Apart from that, how did you get on then, Robert?"

"Lucky for me, it all went well."

"I see your sales were £699.12/- for the week. That's well up on the same week last year."

It was a shock for me to have sales labelled as 'your sales'. That had never occurred to me, but it was a thrill nev-ertheless.

"Every day was busy, and I had a big order from the Soldier's Home at Barry."

"We'll make a greasy grocer of you yet!"

All was well. I had survived a dip in the shallow end of the management pool.

"The salesman tells me you were right to refuse the carrots," the boss told me at the end of Monday. "So never be afraid to refuse bad stock."

As a fortunate diversion from my temporary manage-ment experiences, I was able for a few evenings to spend time with Willie who was back home on leave. I walked along to his house and was quite shocked when I first saw him – he was thinner, and seemed to have lost his normal healthy com-plexion.

"Are you feeling alright?" I enquired.

"Don't know," he said surprisingly. "I become easily tired. I think the knock on the head has done something to me, and I can't get rid of those itchy legs I had when I was last here."

"How much more training are you to get before you get on a real ship?"

"Not long to go now. I can't wait to get off that stonewall frigate."

"What's that?"

"It's the name they give to a shore-based vessel which isn't a real ship, such as HMS *Raleigh* or *Collingwood*."

"Your priority must be to get fit again."

"That's why I was given this special leave."

We spoke about our respective future, but I held back from telling Willie about my opportunity to manage the branch. He seemed to be in such a bad way that I didn't have the heart to mention my progress. We went to the Marine Ballroom on the Saturday evening, just two days before he returned to base.

"Can we go home on an early bus?" he had asked.

I could see he was tired and not his usual ebullient self with his jokes and fun about navy life, so our normal chat about the talent didn't materialise.

On the way home in the bus I tried to brighten Willie's spirits a bit. "Never mind; the dancing in Arbroath is all very well, but it's not as lively as the dancing used to be with Dave Torrie's band at the YMCA in Carnoustie."

"I didn't dance all that much there," said Willie.

"Neither did I," I responded. "That's because when we started to go there on a Saturday night, we used to buy a quarter-pound of sweeties and then, for sixpence, go upstairs to watch the dancing. But we never plucked up courage to dance. Innocent days, Willie!"

As I sat thinking about Willie at home that evening, I was saddened to sense the contrast in our lives at that stage, and when I said goodbye the next day I tried to cheer him up.

"Get a medic to sort you out, Willie – and send me more stories of your dangerous escapades with the girlfriends you have in every port."

"I'll do my best," he said wryly, without his usual jaunty response.

* * *

At the end of June, Mr Munro – while on his routine visit – called me into the boss's office, where I could tell he'd been looking through the ledger books. Suddenly he came out with a blunt statement.

"Well, Robert – you've done well, I believe. How would you like to manage a branch?"

"I don't know if I'm ready for that. Is Mr Stewart leaving?" I said questioningly, thinking he was referring to the Carnoustie shop.

"No, no. It's a branch in Dundee. But don't worry, it's in my area and I'll keep you right," he added reassuringly.

"Which branch, Mr Munro?"

"Brantwood Avenue." I must have looked blank. "That's up the hill at the back of the city," he clarified.

Probably still looking dumbstruck, my mind was in a whirl. I'd been in my own little Carnoustie capsule for the past three and a half years, and cycling to and from the shop. Now it seemed my tiny comfortable world was in for a big shock. How would I manage people I'd never met? Would they work well for a young laddie from Carnoustie? How would I get to and from Dundee every day?

"Think about it, Robert. I'll see you next week."

I had an immediate feeling of walking on air, and then I shuddered at the enormity of the proposition. What a huge step. *After all those years, Mr Munro is going to speak to me next week.*

This was my biggest-ever news item to report to mum, and when I arrived home I found dad there too. I must have been grinning from ear to ear as I rushed into the room.

"I won't be needing my bike now, dad. We can sell it and free up some space in the shed," I said exultantly.

They were sitting in their usual fireside chairs and, in unison, they turned their heads in surprise.

Mum spoke first. In her usual nervous way, she asked me anxiously: "Oh dear. What's gone wrong with you?"

Then dad, anticipating me buying a car: "You can't afford to run a car back and forth to your work."

"I know, but I may be going to work in Dundee."

"Are you being transferred?" mum said disappointedly.

"Well yes, in a way. Mr Munro's offered me the chance to manage a branch, but I'm not sure if I can do it."

"I thought that may happen," dad declared.

Then mum, turning her disappointment into celebration, added her usual logic.

"The company wouldn't offer you that if they didn't think you'd manage. Is it a big branch?" she asked.

"I don't know exactly where it is, or anything about it," I replied.

"Well, Mr Stewart should be able to help you. Can you not ask him? Or even better, ask Mr Munro if you can see the shop," dad suggested.

The next day, I asked the boss about the Brantwood Avenue shop. He hadn't seen it, but he showed me sales increase percentages of each shop in the league table in his office. Brantwood's sales increase was logged at the bottom of the table at three percent.

"It's the smallest branch in Munro's area, and I know the manager there is Jim Campbell. He's a middle-aged man."

Why would Jim Campbell want to leave? I asked myself. *Was there a problem with him or with the branch? Was the shop declining, and did it have staff problems?*

All these questions were in my mind when Mr Munro appeared the following Wednesday seeking my answer.

"Can I see the shop please, before I decide?" I asked Mr Munro with dad's suggestion in mind.

"I'll tell you what, Robert. Meet me at the Overgate branch – that's number thirty-three – at four o'clock on Saturday, and I'll take you to see Brantwood."

CHAPTER 18

Dundee and Brantwood Avenue, or "I'll Take the Job, Mr Munro"

Summer 1960

IT was unreal, and I felt guilty about leaving the boss short-staffed to take off my white coat halfway through a busy Saturday afternoon so that I could jump on an Alexander's Bluebird bus bound for Dundee.

Finding my way to 33 Overgate, Mr Munro's top branch, was easy. I'd looked inside it on my Tuesday afternoon trips to Dundee, and I easily saw that it was an extremely busy shop. The place was packed with Saturday shoppers, with a long queue outside. The window displays were massive, bold, and more striking than Carnoustie branch. The whole scene was one of city vibrancy and clamour. The tempo of staff activity was breathtaking. Voices were loud everywhere, in the street and around the door of "33". It reminded me of market scenes I'd experienced in London. Something was different about the atmosphere. Then I figured that it was the smell of tobacco smoke. The confined area around the shop and the narrow street seemed to hold the smells of grocery and butchery stores invaded by the tobacco odours. In the background, a news-seller was calling out and it took me some time to decipher his call. It was something like "Tully". As I took a short stroll before plucking up courage to enter the shop, I found the source of the loud voice. It was a small, one-legged man wearing a big bonnet and an unseasonal opened raincoat. He appeared to have no teeth and was leaning against a wall, his crutch propped beside him. Then I saw his product: it was the *Dundee Evening Telegraph*. To see him selling that paper at three o'clock in the afternoon was a new experience for me. I strolled back to the branch and noticed, as with the Carnoustie branch, the sun shades were down and the glare from the more powerful lighting seemed magnetic. The Carnoustie shop was well-lit, but this place was glaringly bright and I could see why it was regarded as the company's flagship.

Was the Brantwood branch like this? I trembled slightly, took a deep breath, and joined the queue.

Not wishing to go unannounced into the back shop, I remained in the queue and said – when served – that I had arrived for a meeting with Mr Munro. During a lengthy wait, I took in the whole spectacle. Was it Mr Munro's ploy for me to observe all this? Part of the introduction? If it was, it scared me. All the staff behind the counter looked highly efficient, and I began to see that Carnoustie branch was comparatively tame. Had I been living in a false world? I had another thought: why are none of these switched-on city shop assistants being selected to manage Brantwood? Or worse: have they been offered it and turned it down?

Mr Munro appeared. "Right, Robert – let's go. My car's parked further along the Overgate, near number 123." This, I knew, was another branch further along the street.

With Saturday city shoppers out in force, the Overgate was throbbing with businesses selling all types of products: butchery, clothes, newspapers, shoes, and motorbikes. Opposite number 123, stalls set up on waste ground appeared to do a roaring trade with fish and chips, sweeties and candy-floss being most prominent.

We didn't chat on the journey. I concentrated on the route and the unreal situation. Here I was, sitting beside Mr Munro in his Triumph Mayflower. I could hardly believe it. The same vehicle I used to see parked in Carnoustie, and regarded by me as from another world. Even my boss, I was sure, had never been in this car.

Brantwood Avenue, as earlier indicated by Mr Munro, was in the north of the City with a glimpse of The Law (hill) nearby. The branch looked tiny, and was next door to a Dundee Savings Bank. On the other side was a space for vehicle access to the back door, and beyond that was one of several shops forming a curved avenue of retail businesses. The branch had only one window, and from a distance the front shop appeared to be about a quarter of the size of Carnoustie's selling space.

As we approached the front door, Mr Munro commented: "Here you have to display all canned special offers in one window, along with cooked meats and bacon. You'll see fruit and vegetables can only be displayed and sold from boxes at the doorway."

I was introduced to the manager, Jim Campbell. He looked as my boss had described, but I didn't yet know why he was moving on.

The back shop was half the size of the front area, and on being shown around I noticed a wooden shed – similar in size – was located at the rear. Mr Munro explained that it served as an extension to the back shop.

On close examination I saw that bulk cheese, lard and butter were not offered. Such items were in packets, and there was no sign of a streaky roll.

"We're slowly moving into pre-packed provisions, and we try things out in this branch. We're soon going to stock bags of dried fruits and cereals," said Mr Munro. "In fact, all products will soon be pre-packed."

With low level sales, I realised bulk products wouldn't keep in good condition.

Strangely enough, what seemed out of place was an oversized potato bunker in the back shop, and I remember thinking that pre-packed potatoes would be a positive move in the future. To check on the stock holding capacity, I asked to look inside the shed.

"Any trouble with mice?" I ventured.

"Just keep your eye on it," replied Jim.

That meant a 'yes' to me. Here we go again, I thought.

Returning to the back shop, I asked if I may look inside the fridge – which seemed like a toy compared to Carnoustie's walk-in model.

"Because of space limitation, stock control is more critical here," Jim advised me. It was immediately obvious to me that over-ordering could lead to stock losses.

Based on the chat between Mr Munro and Jim, I gained the certain impression they assumed I would be the new manager. Jim had to deal with customers and my visit, I could sense, was ending.

"Any questions, Robert?" Mr Munro quickly enquired of me.

This prompted me to think back to my Carnoustie experience when there were only three assistants.

"What's the weekly turnover, Mr Munro? I've seen the league table, but it showed only sales percentage increases, not actual sales figures."

"Percentage increases are small here, and sales average about £350 a week. Don't be put off by the size. It keeps three people very busy. The trick is in stock control."

"Yes, I was thinking that," I acknowledged.

"Now, Robert, I live in this area so will you find your way home from here?"

Ah! Another part of the introduction?

"Yes, that's alright," I assured him, in total ignorance of bus stops and timetables.

"Well then, there's a bus stop across the road. Any double or single decker will take you into the centre."

Another first; travelling into the city centre on a green Dundee Corporation double decker. After a short wait for a Bluebird bus, I arrived home just after seven o'clock.

"Well, how did you get on?" mum asked.

"It won't be easy, but I think I could manage it. The shop's small, and must be managed in a different way from the branch here. It's up the hill near The Law, and it looks like it's in a good area."

"You've done well. The company must think you can do it. Do you want to work in the Carnoustie shop all your life?"

That was mum's very clever question, and I knew the answer.

* * *

There had been no mail from Willie for some weeks, and I had been too preoccupied to write. So it was with great surprise that, out of the blue one evening, he appeared at our door.

Mum and dad greeted him, and we chatted about his journey. When I asked him about his on-going medical assistance he was receiving, he stunned us.

"I've got bad news. I'm out of the navy," he said, looking at the floor.

"Gee, that is bad news, Willie. Can you not get leave to help you get fit again?"

"No, they can't carry passengers like me, and all my mates will be moving on now. I'm not going to finish my training course."

"That's a shame, William," mum said sympathetically. "Have they said what's wrong with you?"

"I've been invalided out because I've got something called Hodgkin's Disease."

"Can you not be cured and get back in to the Navy?" I asked, although it seemed unlikely.

"I don't know. Maybe it will be a long time before I'm better."

I didn't want to make a big thing of it, but I told Willie how my chance had come along to manage a branch in Dundee. I explained that I wouldn't be around so much in Carnoustie, though we could meet up at week-ends. We agreed to keep in touch, but with my onerous working hours there seemed little chance of spending as much time together as we previously had. He told me not to worry about that, but that he would enjoy getting out and about sometime. When Willie left, we all felt very subdued at his plight.

"He didn't look well, and he's lost his zest," mum noted gloomily.

One sunny warm Sunday afternoon – along with my friend Tom, who taught me how to drive – I took Willie for a drive to Arbroath, and we parked at Victoria Park. I suggested a walk along the promenade, but Willie remained shivering in the back seat with his mum's blanket wrapped around him. It was then that I realised Willie had a serious condition.

There seemed little point in leaving Willie uncomfortable, so we drove back to Carnoustie and went for a hot orange in the Beach Café. Some girls we knew stopped to chat, and when asked why he was on leave again Willie explained that he'd left the Navy as he was unfit.

"What's wrong?" asked Maureen, who was studying to be a nurse.

"I don't really know," Willie said. "Something called Hodgkin's Disease."

"Well, I've just been revising for my exams, so have a look in this textbook while I order a coffee."

Willie went to the index and looked up the page, and I peered over his shoulder to read a bold heading: "Hodgkins Disease – an incurable condition which mainly affects healthy young males."

Neither of us read any more, and Willie shut the book. When Maureen came back and asked if we'd found an answer, Tom winked at her and simply said that she should read it when she gets the chance.

Nothing more was ever said between us on the subject again, and all I could do was visit Willie when I got the chance. When I went home and told mum and dad, we were all shocked and saddened. I felt ill at my inability to help Willie, and went to lie down on my bed. I found myself reflecting on the bittersweet good days that Willie and I had shared in recent times. Questions turned over in my mind. *Would this have happened if he hadn't joined the navy? Were the itchy legs a symptom, and the blow on his head a cause? What's going on in Willie's head, and how can I realistically help him?* Looking back at that sad time, I realise how ill-equipped I was to handle the situation, and consequently found it impossible to help Willie.

* * *

Mr Munro visited the following Wednesday.

"Well, Robert? What do you think?" he said with a twinkle in his eye.

"I'll take the job, Mr Munro," I replied without hesitation, intending to reflect my positive decision.

"Well done. Your pay will be £18 a week, and you'll get half-year profit bonuses depending on your stock results. What do you think about that?"

"That's fine, Mr Munro," I said, folding my arms and smiling.

This would more than double my current wage, and I saw for the first time why the boss was so keen to look after every penny from his tomato boxes and empty bottles. It was all part of building his bonus.

By chance, the following day I met Jock.

"How's it going, Robbie? Still selling all that cheap bulk stuff?" he said in his characteristic cheeky way.

"Aye, but not for long. I'll be selling quality provisions in packets soon," I replied triumphantly.

"Oh, moving into the high-class grocery and wines and spirits market, are we?" he teased.

"No. I'm going to be managing a branch in Dundee, and just like you I'll be selling quality provisions in packets," I proudly announced.

"Seriously?"

"Yes, Jock. I'm moving into the big city scene," I said with a wide grin.

CHAPTER 19

Farewell Carnoustie, or "He's a Wee Greasy Grocer After All"

Summer 1960

THE blinds were down, and the boss was standing in his usual spot near the till counting money. I was tidying the contents in the provisions window, and the ladies were sweeping up behind the counters and washing display stands and marble tops. It was my last Saturday evening in Carnoustie branch; the end of another busy day, and I was leaving my colleagues at the height of the holiday season.

I remember thinking it felt normal, yet it was to end. A chapter was closing, and part of me wanted to hold on to it. Yet I knew I must progress. My comfort zone was ending, and I had some nervousness about my move to Brantwood.

As usual the boss and I were still tidying and the ladies, having finished their last chores, were exiting through the front shop. One by one the boss handed over pay packets as they passed. Staffing level had increased to seven, and everyone wished me well as they walked out. No special gathering. No speeches. No show of emotions, and I was thankful for some normality.

"All the best!" chorused Cathie, Izzy and Dot as they stood together.

"Thanks!" was all I could say. Those three had been my trainers, mentors and friends, and I owed a lot to them.

"He's a wee greasy grocer after all!" the boss called out humorously, and they all laughed.

It's only by looking back after many years that I realise how much my life had been nurtured in that shop. I didn't have the words nor the time then to verbalise it, but I had learned so much that would help to set me on a path for the future. I certainly wasn't aware then of a thing called a career path. In no particular order, I learned valuable lessons about my discipline towards work and people, especially customers. Then there was the need for accuracy, common sense and reliability. Oh yes, and a good memory, because cans and packets didn't have a price marked on them in those days – that had to be remembered.

Within these four walls I had learned my merchant skills – my craft – and where I had gained my fledgling business knowledge and, perhaps more importantly, a period within which I wittingly or unwittingly discovered correct attitudes in many aspects. I think my retail experience presented to me the fact that life was a balance of profits, losses, quality, value, courtesy, and setting a balance between the needs of the company, the shop, and the individuals.

The boss's anticipated "Go, go, greasy grocer go" follow-up didn't come. Did he think his magic spell had worked?

***

On that first July Monday morning, on board a double-decker Alexander's bus, I asked for a six-day return ticket. My recollection is that the cost was about seven and sixpence, and by the time I had twelve holes punched in it I hoped I would be definite in my mind about starting at Brantwood – although I had no intention of admitting defeat, as this was a significant step in my life. On my route I saw Annfield Cottage, where I spent my early childhood years with memories of German bombers, marching pipe bands, pet rabbits, mice or rats in the loft, and Barry school and church – all reminders of my very early life. Then the bus, by chance, stopped momentarily outside the bungalow where I was born, and I had time to think of what mum and dad had done for me. Westhaven was in another direction, but it too had been a wonderful part of growing up.

While thinking of more recent events, my mind went back to that evening when I parked my bike and looked in to ask the boss if I could start as an apprentice. Now here I was on my way to be a manager. Soon I would have shop keys, and the responsibilities that went with them. As I travelled on, I looked back to my apprenticeship years; they had become easier as time moved on, but now I was going into unknown, uncharted waters. No one, so far, had told me how to be a manager: the do's and the don'ts. All I had was one example: Mr Stewart with his "Go, go, greasy grocer go" mantra, his humour, and his leadership.

My morning journeys to Brantwood Avenue, I discovered, were easy. Leave Carnoustie at seven fifteen, arrive at Seagate. Walk to Wellgate as advised by Mr Munro, then climb the famous steps to Victoria Road. There I could take a number 1, 1a or 1b bus to a stop near the branch. My return home in the evening was a route via the city centre where, as a favour for Jim, I deposited the cash takings in the Royal Bank of Scotland night safe in Reform Street. By the time I'd closed at six o'clock, counted the cash, done the paperwork (checked by Jim) and been to the bank, it was time for my bus to Carnoustie, arriving home at seven thirty. No mobile phones in those days to warn mum I would be late, but I made an impulse decision to look in to see Willie. It was a good decision, but one which shook me to the core when I saw him wrapped in a blanket while sitting beside a coal fire. I immediately felt I was intruding on a personal tragedy, and that I was a fraud – while he was in dire trouble, my life was moving on. We couldn't say much as Willie was so weak, and as his mum came to the door to see me off she was in tears.

"He's had a very bad day. He watched *The Flying Doctor*, that Australian programme, and it followed the story of a young man who died from Hodgkin's Disease."

None of my good fortune meant anything to me when I saw and felt Willie's plight that evening. I seemed to be on a fairground ride that I couldn't get off, and yet poor Willie was going nowhere. There was no justice.

* * *

On the first day, Jim introduced me to Pud – the bright and outgoing message laddie – and to Winnie, the quiet-natured staff member. My first week with Jim was immediately prior to the Dundee August holiday fortnight. During that time I had a shock. I'd served a customer and gone through the usual routines, although I faltered my way with little knowledge of stock location. Jim had welcomed her with a cheery hello, so I guessed she must have been a regular. Likewise he bid her a courteous goodbye.

"Do you know who that was?" he asked me with a broad grin.

"No," I replied innocently.

"That was Munro's wife!" Jim announced loudly.

"What?"

"Yes, they live just across the other side of Strathmore Avenue."

"Oh yes. I remember Mr Munro saying that."

"She's normal. Nothing to worry about," he reassured me.

My instinct told me that Mr Munro had probably asked her to shop and check out the new boy manager, and more importantly to find out if he was charging at the right prices.

Another amazing experience. A journey in the Triumph Mayflower, and now his wife is one of my customers. What would my workmates in Carnoustie think of that?

The Thursday in that week was unforgettable. Workers on packed buses were already celebrating the start of their holiday. I could see that more than a few men seemed to have spent a lot of their holiday pay to celebrate the event with a few drams. (Probably more than a few.) Good luck to them, I thought; they seem to work hard here. This city was my new world – a place where I had gone to night classes and to shop or to watch wrestling, but rather scary for me now as a place to work. There were times when I couldn't follow what people were saying. Not only what they said, but also how they spoke.

"Gie me a luppie o' tatties, son."

I was amused at still being described a 'son', but I'd no idea what a 'luppie' was.

I went to the potato bin in the back shop and Winnie, who had witnessed my blank look, came to explain.

"What's a luppie, Winnie ?" I said anxiously before she spoke.

"That's seven pounds. But it's really a 'lippe', not a 'luppie'."

Ah well – when in Rome.

Another confusion for me related to bread: a pan or a plain loaf in Carnoustie was one piece of bread, i.e. a loaf, but in Dundee it was a half loaf. Although feeling like a country bumpkin in the big city, it was exciting and friendly – and yet I had an ever-present wariness for the unexpected.

One of my first impressions on these bright sunny July mornings was of the apparent high level of unemployment in the city. This was because I constantly saw a group of middle-aged and elderly men loitering at the lower end of the Well-gate. They looked quite poor and rough-clad.

Feeling quite sorry for them, I mentioned this to Jim.

"Ah yes, Robert – they're carters. Men who are seeking casual work as lorry driver mates."

"It always seems to be the same men."

"Yes, they probably are. They work on a one-off daily basis. Probably do a run somewhere in Scotland and be back by evening."

"Why can't they be given a regular job?" I asked sympathetically.

"Companies in the city don't have a constant need for transport workers. It's mainly jute lorries which pick up bales of jute at the harbour as and when ships arrive, then distribute around Angus. The drivers look for a mate to help. Some, but not all, will find work. If not, they'll pick up unemploy-ment benefit."

It was another piece of information about Dundee city life.

We took stock on the Saturday night, and Jim handed me the keys of my very own branch. He had told me he was moving on to manage one of the two Forfar branches as he wanted to be nearer his family.

"All the best in Forfar, Jim," I volunteered.

"Thanks, Robert. Good luck in Brantwood. Remember to get your lippes and loafs right," he said with a grin.

Here I was, talking on equal terms with another branch manager. I couldn't believe it. I was about three months short of my twentieth birthday, and Mr Munro had told me I was the company's youngest ever manager. Business was very qui-et during the Dundee holiday fortnight – a well-timed intro-duction for me by Mr Munro?

* * *

The early morning sun shone directly on to the front of the shop and, when I opened the door each morning, I met the powerful aroma of tomatoes. This was a peak selling period, and in the confines of the small shop the sweet, pungent, minty air had built up and caught my nostrils. In a strange way it was a positive injection for me, and a similar experience when I used to enter the Carnoustie shop. Somehow it was the comforting smell of business as usual. Routines developed: bus travel, banking, shop procedures, and managing two staff plus a message laddie. I quickly learned that, whether by de-sign or chance, the branch was uniquely positioned geograph-ically. The shop served three distinct categories of customers:

an up-market, well-off section on the north side of Strathmore Avenue; customers from the well maintained and tidy 'Glens' council house scheme; as well as people from the nearby Beechwood housing estate. The last group consisted of working wives trying to make ends meet, as well as rather poor-looking pensioners. Some of those hard-working housewives worked in a jute mill in the city centre, got off a bus, shopped at my branch, then walked the half-mile home. Some asked for a delivery by the message laddie.

"That's awfi guid o' you, son," Mrs Reilly would say. "I'll manage okay if you can send your laddie wi' the rest."

Despite their undoubted hard and dirty work, they were always cheery. With jute dust covering their hair and clothing, they nevertheless livened the place up.

In my ignorance, I asked one lady: "Your nose is bleeding! Have you had an accident?" I was genuinely concerned.

"Naw, it'll be the snuff!" she replied in a matter-of-fact way.

In contrast, there was one 'posh' customer who regularly asked me to put a can of salmon in a paper bag so that her dog wouldn't see the label as she popped the can into her shopping basket. Posh dog too!

One evening, a well-off customer – Mrs McLaren – parked her car outside the shop and caused a stir. She was driving the first Morris 'Mini' car any of us had seen! It was this event which highlighted a subtle change in the relationship between customers and staff in Dundee compared to Carnoustie, because Pud the message laddie – who carried groceries out to Mrs McLaren's car – casually engaged in a chat about the vehicle and then was invited to sit in the driving seat. With no other customers in the shop at that moment, I too went out to the car and was invited to have a close inspection of this novel vehicle that was new on the market. This was an example of a welcome and more relaxed culture than I'd experienced in Carnoustie.

Mr Munro looked in weekly, and was always supportive. Several weeks into my new job, he had a shock when he found I had personally gone out on the message bike to Beechwood and successfully collected debt which he had previously written off in my accounts. That was immediate profit for my branch. My old boss's advice and the profit bonus scheme were never out of my thoughts. My attitudes to debt and the misery inflicted by it was now a different matter.

Winter came and I purchased a second-hand Ford Prefect car, enjoying a beneficial change in my daily routines. Gone was the rush for buses, as I now had flexibility and my working day was shorter. Apart from half-day, the shop closed for lunch at one o'clock for one and a quarter hours. In those days I could park in Reform Street, collect the bank bag, and pick up change for the till. One of the tellers was Bill McGregor, my former classmate. We both left school aged fifteen and he had been school dux, but here we were at the age of nineteen – Bill a banker and me a shop manager. While he was counting my bank notes, I teased him and received a justified response.

"You know, Bill, I make all this money and you only have to count it."

"Yes, Robbie; I'm the one who knows how to keep it safe and where to invest it."

We talked about our friend Willie, and said how powerless we felt. We agreed to look in to see him soon. I had been feeling guilty about getting home so late in the evenings, and had not visited as much as I should have.

One day I met Mr Leitch, my old teacher at the college. He was very interested in my progress. He told me the Grocers' Institute had removed product knowledge from the curriculum, bringing an end to the practical examinations in London.

One big breakthrough for me was to attend branch managers' meetings. I remember the venue for my first gathering was in St Andrews, and the meeting lasted a day. My old boss approached me.

"So, how's the wee greasy grocer getting on in the big city?" he said, staring at me with his big eyes.

"Trying to look after all the pennies, just like you taught me!" I boasted.

I picked up all the chat and jokes between the managers. Even Mr Munro was telling risqué stories. I couldn't believe it. A new world, sure enough. It gave me a lot of confidence to feel part of this group of experienced and robust managers.

When my old boss had shown me the branch league table, I had noticed Brantwood Avenue was at the bottom of the list with a three percent increase in sales. I had made a mental note and aimed to see Brantwood Avenue climb the table. Gradually, I did manage to get to second top with an eighteen percent increase.

"So the wee greasy grocer's making his way to the top of the league now!" my old boss said when I visited Carnoustie branch one half-day Wednesday afternoon.

On receiving word that we should visit our friend Willie urgently, Bill and I looked in to see him on a Sunday morning. But it was too late. He had passed away in the early hours.

"He died the hard way," were his dad's words, which I will never forget. We had lost a pal who was not yet twenty-one years old. It just was not fair: Bill and I were happily progressing, and Willie had not had time for success. There were no words to describe my loss.

* * *

Mr Munro must have been suitably impressed with my attempts. After eighteen months of running the Brantwood shop, I was surprised one day when he said casually – during one of his visits – that he had some good news for me.

"Let's step out to the shed for a minute," he said quietly.

We did so, and then – as he packed some notes into his attaché case – he asked me: "How do you fancy managing a bigger shop, Robert?"

"That sounds very interesting, Mr Munro. Which branch?" I enquired, trying to sound business-like.

"There've been a few changes in my territory, and the Logie Street branch in Lochee needs a replacement manager. Are you up for it?"

"Can I see the shop before I decide?" dad's old advice came to mind. It seemed like I'd said those words just a few months previously.

"Of course you can. Meet me there after you close tonight. Do you know where it is?"

"Yes. Opposite the church."

"The move won't happen for another month or so," he told me.

I visited Logie Street, and immediately saw the space and potential. The shop floor area was about the size of the Carnoustie branch. I confirmed that I would accept the offer.

"Well done, Robert. It's a great step for your future," he said convincingly as we chatted in the back shop.

It had one checkout, and was described as an experimental self-selection store. One step towards self-service.

In one month I'd be moving on.

CHAPTER 20

Looking Back, or "Remember, Jim – It All Started in Our Playground!"

1962

THE prospect of moving on inspired me to take stock of what I had done and the changes in the trade I had witnessed in only a few years.

I was about to move to a self-selection branch with counter areas only at provisions and fruit and vegetables. I didn't realise it then but – as we now know – specialist counters selling fish and butchery would become an everyday part of supermarket retailing, thus removing almost all of those small retailers from the high streets. Already the latest store in Lochee High Street, Dundee, was self-service. It was only a matter of time until all stores would be converted. Most of my old skills would no longer be required, as dealing directly with customers on such a scale would end. Skinning cheeses, opening butter barrels and dealing with seventy-pound boxes of dates would cease, as these products – like everything else – would be stocked in packets. No more handling mucky potatoes and cold meats. No more greasy hands to be constantly washed. Using a garden hoe to scrape grease off the floor would be a skill of the past. Generally, in future all unwrapped or loose foods such as cheese, butter, and cooked meats would be in packets, and more hygienically handled. Gone were the days of handling loose sweets and biscuits so that, for example, my former science teacher Miss Fleming could now pick up a wire basket and choose whatever biscuits she wished then go to a checkout. Her former pupil wouldn't be handling her food, and she would find chocolate vermicelli on a shelf all on her own without embarrassment.

New shopping methods would make it easier for staff and customers. Time-saving convenience foods were being introduced almost weekly. Not only was shopping easier, but housewives would find new products that would reduce chores in the kitchen as preparation time would be reduced.

I looked back at my time on a message bike; the dangerous missions in all weathers and the strange deliveries I had to make. Trips to the jam factory, the Soldier's Home, the agonising Monday delivery to the foundry canteen, and collecting lettuce from Mr McKenzie were now all in the past. The silly duties such as swapping cans of soup and setting mouse traps were all in a bygone age. My apprentice days – when I learned so many aspects of the business – seemed to have flown by, and effortlessly brought me to Dundee and to management. It seemed that almost overnight my personal world was coincidentally changing with new practices in the trade. It was an amazing parallel, and little did I think then that the new, emerging grocery world would develop to become the giant supermarkets we see today. Nor did I imagine that the message boys would be replaced by vans delivering groceries ordered by customers on a computer.

Mr Leitch had already told me tea tasting and coffee roasting were now off the Grocers' Institute syllabus, and although I was no longer studying I was certain night class subjects must have altered and developed to reflect new changes.

My grocery introduction had started in my school playground, when Jim – who initially handed me a job as a butcher's boy – was instrumental in finding me a more suitable job as a message laddie. Luckily for me, I experienced a brief spark into the world of radio and television engineering which gave me the insight into my own personality and turned me back to the busy excitement of grocery retailing. Who knows – perhaps the Vikings shaped my future? Strangely, the new technical world I thought was a job for the future is no longer around, as radio and television engineers are now extinct. It was my school friend, Alan Craigie, who inadvertently helped me discover that the grocery world was my best personality fit.

My friends had told me Bill McGregor had, on completion of his banking studies, secured a banking post in India and they were all agog – as I was – that he was offered a salary of one thousand pounds per year. It hadn't occurred to me, but my own impending move would give me membership of the 'over a thousand per annum' club, which was a much-discussed objective amongst my peers in those days.

One afternoon about a week before I left Brantwood branch, and as if by some magical force, while I was setting up a vegetable display at the front door of the shop Alan Craigie stepped out of his van to speak with me. He'd no idea where I worked; he had just spotted me at the doorway as he was driving along.

"So, this is where you are? I'd heard you were in Dundee now."

"Yes, I left your world of valves and condensers a long time ago. What are you doing these days?"

"I'm a time served radio and TV engineer now, and I work in Dundee."

"Has it all worked out alright for you then, Alan?"

"Yes. I finished my college course, but the pay's not great, Robbie. Did you make the right decision?" I detected some dismay in his voice.

"So far! There's lots of change going on in the grocery world, and I've just been offered a bigger branch at Logie Street."

"That's brilliant, Robbie! I'll look in and see you now and again."

When Alan drove off I was left with a mixture of feelings. He conveyed a hint of sadness, and I sensed disappointment in his voice. It seemed to me that he was not perfectly happy. It was quite odd, because the new, exciting and glamorous commercial world of selling television sets seemed to be at odds with the role of a TV engineer. In contrast, my thoughts were brighter and more expansive, as changes in my trade seemed to bring wider and better jobs and careers which confirmed to me that – fortunately – I had made a good decision. A few years later, Alan left the television repair job and moved into the micro-electronics industry, where he had a successful career in the UK and South Africa.

With the prospect of advancement, I remember taking time to reflect on my life in general, and my overwhelming memory was then realising how luck had played a part. My parents had given me a caring and loving introduction into the world. They instilled in me the need for careful spending, honesty, respect for others, and diligence in my work. But I had more luck by pure chance: meeting Jim, my boyhood guide and mentor; the opportunity to discover where my true work fulfilment lay; the influence of my boss and Mr Munro; and the availability of further education. Even the Vikings had a hand (or an oar) in my luck, and the way that – simply because a cinema was showing a poor film on a certain evening – I accidentally stumbled into amateur drama, which was an unwitting way of gaining some confidence.

Another amazing surprise was to come.

One day, a policeman got off his bike and approached the shop. It was Jim! The same person who had told me about the Willie Low's message boy job.

"Where have you been, Jim? And what are you doing here?"

"I've been in the Scots Guards, and now I'm in Dundee. How are you getting on, Robbie?"

"Fine. I'm manager here, and I'm moving on next week to a branch at Logie Street." I wasn't boasting, but I couldn't stop telling friends my good news. We reminisced about Westhaven and our young days for several minutes.

"Do you remember fishing for dargies and looking after the boats at the harbour, Robbie?"

"Unforgettable! And what about the porpoises, the partons, and the day we nearly lost Ollie?" ('Partons' was a local term for edible crabs.)

"Aye, you're right. Ollie could have been sucked under by his wellies."

"And Jim, what about those great nights at the ballaster – cricket, fireworks and bonfires? I wonder what Donald

Ford's doing these days? He's probably a super-duper cricketer by now."

"Aye, Robbie. And what about the night your mum was chased by a rocket?" he laughed out loud.

"She was famous, Jim! She got her name in *The Sunday Post*."

"Aye, great days."

We chatted about the wonderful times we'd had, and how lucky we'd both been.

"I'll look in and see you now and again."

"That's great. Remember – you started it all, that day in the playground back in 1953!"

POSTSCRIPT

I don't see message laddies on bikes with big baskets these days, but I do see supermarket van drivers essentially doing the same job as I did.

The grassy ballaster valley is no more, as it's been levelled by the Council. The Coastguard training 'mast' has gone, and so too have all the 'Coasties'. No swings, no beach hut, and upturned boats are no more – not even a scorch mark of a recent bonfire. The harbour and the marker poles are still there, as are 'Limpy, Dargie and Poddlie', but I don't see lines of boys fishing from them, and I guess very few people today will know the names we gave them and the fun we had on those magic rocks in my wonderland world of Westhaven.

You may like to know that I still keep in touch with Jim who, after all those years, is still able to reel off the names of every boat owner at Westhaven. Bill came back from his 25 year banking career in India, and we occasionally meet for a chat about the 'old days'. When Jock comes on holiday to Carnoustie from his home in England, we play golf and reminisce about our friendly rivalry – and I must admit, his golf is of better quality than mine.

Dad died at the age of 86, and mum passed away in 2015 in her 101st year.

APPENDIX I

PRE-DECIMAL BRITISH CURRENCY

Farthing = 1/4 penny
Halfpenny ('ha'penny') = 1/2 penny
Penny ('copper') = one pence (1d)
Threepence ('thruppenny bit') = 3 pence
Sixpence ('tanner') = 6 pence
Shilling = 12 pence (1s)
Florin = 2 shillings
Half Crown = 2 shillings and 6 pence
Crown = 5 shillings = 1/4 pound
Pound = 20 shillings = 240 pence (£1)
Sovereign = face value of £1 (approx .24 oz. of 22 carat gold).

APPENDIX II

IMPERIAL TO DECIMAL CURRENCY CONVERSION TABLE

12 old pennies (d) = 1 shilling (s) = 5 new pence
1 florin = 2 shillings = 10 new pence
1 half crown = 2 shillings and sixpence = 12½ new pence
1 crown = 5 shillings = two half crowns = 25 new pence
1 pound (£) = 20 shillings = 240 old pennies = 100 new pence

ILLUSTRATIONS

Barry, near Carnoustie; the house where the author
was born is on the left, and Barry East Church
(which the Murray family attended) is on the right

Westhaven

Granny and grandad's croft cottage in Dunninald

Mum and dad with infant Robbie and Peem (James)
at Granny Taylor's croft cottage

Peem, Isobel and
Robbie

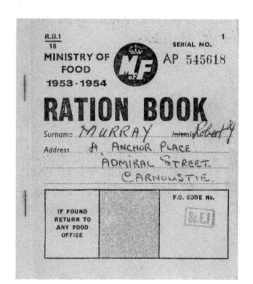

Robbie's ration
book

Anchor Place, Admiral Street, Westhaven
(in the present day)

Robbie on his way
home from school (his
brother Peem and pal
Ollie in the back-
ground)

Robbie on his tricycle near Carnoustie bandstand (now demolished)

Robbie, Isobel and Peem on the putting green, with Carnoustie golf course starter's box and Carnoustie bandstand in the background

Murray family photo from the 1950s

Peem, Isobel and Robbie,
dressed for a Cub Scout meeting

A Murray family day
out at Carnoustie
Beach

Shopping
in Carnoustie;
dad is carrying a
brand new Vidor
dry (radio) battery

A family holiday to Greenock to stay with
an aunt and uncle

On a caravan holiday in Dunkeld (the same holiday
where Robbie would need rescuing from a well)

Carnoustie 2nd Troop Boy Scouts;
Robbie is in the front row on the far right

Patrol Leader Robbie at Camp Glenfarg

The Coastguard Lookout Station at Westhaven

Carnoustie School

Family day out on a Clyde steamer

Dad wearing
his railway uniform

Carnoustie Railway Station in the 1950s;
the John Menzies & Co. Ltd. newspaper kiosk is
visible on the right hand side of both shots

(Images reproduced by kind courtesy of Ian Foulis
of the Angus Railway Group)

Part of the ballaster (now levelled)

Peem with his new bike, following the run to
Dunninald, Montrose

Staying at the guest house in Jersey, during a family holiday to the Channel Islands

At the entrance to the German underground hospital on Jersey

Shamrock Street, Carnoustie;
the Murray family home from 1955

Robbie on his motorbike

Mum, dad and 'Baby' Jean
borrow Robbie's motorbike

WM. LOW & COMPANY LIMITED

News Letter

BELLFIELD STREET, DUNDEE 9th SEPTEMBER, 1960

Staff Changes

Mr J. Campbell, manager at Brantwood Avenue, Dundee
branch has been appointed manager at Castle Street, Forfar,
and Mr R. Murray, provision hand at Carnoustie has been
appointed manager at Brantwood Avenue.

Detail from the official Wm Low & Co. Ltd.
Newsletter for 9th September 1960, announcing
Robbie's promotion to manager of the Brantwood
Avenue branch in Dundee

A Wolseley car, similar to the one bought by Robbie
for £27

A Triumph Mayflower car, similar to the one driven
by Mr Munro

Mum and dad's
Golden Wedding
Anniversary
photo

Mum on the
occasion of her 100th
birthday

ACKNOWLEDGEMENTS

With grateful thanks to:

All my friends in Tay Writers, Dundee, who helped me so much in the early stages of my book.

My brother James (aka Peem) for his sketches.

Catriona Leslie for her input into my early chapters.

Eddie Small, Dundee University, for his guidance and encouragement.

Members of Angus Writing Circle for their valued support.

Ian Foulis of Angus Railway Group, for kind permission to use historical photographs supplied by the organisation.

Montrose Museum, Angus, for use of an exact look-a-like message bike.

'House of Memories', Monifieth, Angus, and the 'Harbour Nights Guest House', Arbroath, for permission to photograph authentic items.

Elaine for her photography and forbearance.

Extremis Publishing Ltd., Stirling, for their faith and trust in my work.

And all the characters in this book, without whom there would be no story.

ABOUT THE AUTHOR

Robert Taylor Murray was born in Barry, near Carnoustie, in 1940. Growing up in Westhaven and later residing in Carnoustie itself, he attended Barry and Carnoustie Schools before becoming an apprentice grocer with William Low & Company Ltd. He qualified as a Member of The Grocers' Institute, and was appointed manager of William Low's Brantwood branch in Dundee, becoming the company's youngest ever manager at the age of 19. He later oversaw the Logie Street branch in Lochee.

Robert went on to manage a larger third branch in Dundee and then, after attending further education management courses, discovered he was sufficiently qualified to successfully apply for a post as a lecturer in distributive trades subjects at Dundee Commercial College – a position he held for five years. Realising how much the retail trade was changing and feeling he was less in touch to reflect the current scene, he applied to join The Grocers' Institute and was appointed Training Development Officer for part of London and east England, where he advised companies and colleges on training in the retail grocery trade.

After two years he returned to the Dundee area when he was appointed Training Officer for Watson & Philip, a national wholesale food distributor. He remained with that company for thirty-three years, during which time he was appointed Personnel Manager and eventually became Group Personnel Manager with responsibility for three thousand employees and, latterly, in the London area.

Following a company acquisition he became redundant at the age of sixty-two. In retirement he has again been actively involved in amateur theatre. He is a member of Tay Writers – a Dundee based writing group – and Angus Writers' Circle, and writes short stories. He has written a stage presentation on the life of Robert Burns, *The Spirit of Robbie Burns*, which has been performed several times by amateurs in Tayside and details of which are available world-wide on the Internet at *www.spiritrobbieburns.com*.

He has two daughters, each married, and four grandchildren.

When he is not writing, he enjoys travelling, hill walking and golfing.

An Innocent Abroad

The Misadventures of an Exchange Teacher in Montana

By David M. Addison

When, in 1978, taking a bold step into the unknown, the author, accompanied by his wife and young family, swapped his boring existence in Grangemouth in central Scotland for life in Missoula, Montana, in the western United States, he could never have foreseen just how much of a life-changing experience it would turn out to be.

As an exchange teacher, he was prepared for a less formal atmosphere in the classroom, while, for their part, his students had been warned that he would be "Mr Strict". It was not long before this clash of cultures reared its ugly head and the author found life far more "exciting" than he had bargained for. Within a matter of days of taking up his post, he found himself harangued in public by an irate parent, while another reported him to the principal for "corrupting" young minds.

Outwith the classroom, he found daily life just as shocking. Lulled by a common language into a false sense of a "lack of foreignness", he was totally unprepared for the series of culture shocks that awaited him from the moment he stepped into his home for the year – the house from *Psycho*.

There were times when he wished he had stayed at home in his boring but safe existence in Scotland, but mainly this is a heart-warming and humorous tale of how this Innocent abroad, reeling from one surprising event to the next, gradually begins to adapt to his new life. And thanks to a whole array of colourful personalities and kind people (hostile parents not withstanding), he finally comes to realise that this exchange was the best thing he had ever done.

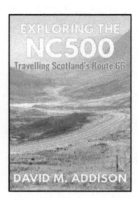

Exploring the NC500

Travelling Scotland's Route 66

By David M. Addison

Travelling anti-clockwise, David M. Addison seeks his kicks on Scotland's equivalent of Route 66. Otherwise known as NC500, the route takes you through five hundred miles of some of Scotland's most spectacular scenery. No wonder it has been voted as one of the world's five most scenic road journeys.

There are many ways of exploring the NC500. You can drive it, cycle it, motorbike it or even walk it, even if you are not one of The Proclaimers! And there are as many activities, places of interest and sights to be seen along the way as there are miles.

This is a personal account of the author's exploration of the NC500 as well as some detours from it, such as to the Black Isle, Strathpeffer and Dingwall. Whatever your reason or reasons for exploring the NC500 may be, you should read this book before you go, or take it with you as a *vade mecum*. It will enhance your appreciation of the NC500 as you learn about the history behind the turbulent past of the many castles; hear folk tales, myths and legends connected with the area; become acquainted with the ancient peoples who once lived in this timeless landscape, and read about the lives of more recent heroes such as the good Hugh Miller who met a tragic end and villains such as the notorious Duke of Sutherland, who died in his bed (and may not be quite as bad as he is painted). There are a good number of other characters too of whom you may have never heard: some colourful, some eccentric, some *very* eccentric.

You may not necessarily wish to follow in the author's footsteps in all that he did, but if you read this book you will certainly see the landscape through more informed eyes as you do whatever you want to do *en route* NC500.

Sit in your car and enjoy the scenery for its own sake (and remember you get a different perspective from a different direction, so you may want to come back and do it again to get an alternative point of view!), or get out and explore it at closer quarters – the choice is yours, but this book will complement your experience, whatever you decide.

Planes on Film
Ten Favourite Aviation Films

By Colin M. Barron

One of the most durable genres in cinema, the aviation film has captivated audiences for decades with tales of heroism, bravery and overcoming seemingly insurmountable odds. Some of these movies have become national icons, achieving critical and commercial success when first released in cinemas and still attracting new audiences today.

In *Planes on Film: Ten Favourite Aviation Films*, Colin M. Barron reveals many little-known facts about the making of several aviation epics. Every movie is discussed in comprehensive detail, including a thorough analysis of the action and a complete listing of all the aircraft involved. With information about where the various planes were obtained from and their current location, the book also explores the subject of aviation films which were proposed but ultimately never saw the light of day.

With illustrations and meticulous factual commentary, *Planes on Film* is a book which will appeal to aviation enthusiasts, military historians and anyone who has an interest in cinema. Written by an author with a lifelong passion for aircraft and their depiction on the silver screen, *Planes on Film* presents a lively and thought-provoking discourse on a carefully-chosen selection of movies which have been drawn from right across the history of this fascinating cinematic genre.

Battles on Screen
World War II Action Movies

By Colin M. Barron

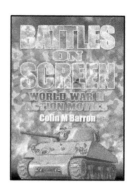

The Second World War was one of the defining historical events of the Twentieth Century. This global conflict was responsible for enormous trials and great heroism, and the horrors and gallantry that it inspired has formed the basis of some of the most striking movies ever committed to celluloid.

From the author of *Planes on Film*, *Battles on Screen* offers both an analysis and celebration of cinema's engagement with World War II, discussing the actors, the locations, the vehicles and the production teams responsible for bringing these epics to life. Reaching across the decades, the impact and effectiveness of many classic war films are examined in detail, complete with full listings of their cast and crew.

Ranging from the real–life figures and historical events which lay behind many of these features to the behind-the-scenes challenges which confronted the film crews at the time of their production, *Battles on Screen* contains facts, statistics and critical commentary to satisfy even the most stalwart fan of the war movie genre.

Also Available from Extremis Publishing

The Fearn Bobby
Reflections from a Life in Scottish Policing

By Ian McNeish

'It's all about the community', the words of Kenneth Ross, Chief Constable of Ross and Sutherland Constabulary, guided Ian McNeish through thirty years of police service. They were true then, back in 1974, and they are true now.

Ian held a police warrant card for three decades, serving communities across Scotland. In that time, his work saw him moving from the northerly constabulary where he policed the rural Hill of Fearn to the social challenges that presented themselves amongst the urban landscape of Central Scotland.

From his formative years in post-War Scotland through to his application to join the police service, Ian has led a rich and varied professional life that ranged from working in iron foundries to building electronic parts for the Kestrel Jump Jet and legendary Concorde aircraft. But once he had joined the police service, he found himself faced with a whole new range of life-changing experiences – some of them surprising, a few even shocking, but all of them memorable.

Leading the reader through his involvement in front line situations, Ian explains the effects of anti-social behaviour and attending criminal court appearances, in addition to dealing with death and the responsibilities of informing those left behind. He considers topics such as ethics, public interest, police and firearms, drug issues, causes of crime, and a lot more besides.

In a career where his duties ranged from policing national strikes to providing comfort and support through personal tragedies, Ian advanced through the ranks and saw first-hand the vital importance of effective management and good teamwork. Whether as the 'Fearn Bobby', policing a remote countryside outpost, as a seconded officer working for the Chief Executive of a Regional Council, or as a Local Unit Commander in Bo'ness, Ian always knew the importance of putting the community first. Comparing today's policing techniques with his own professional experiences and examining both the good times and the harrowing pitfalls of the job, his account of life in the force is heartfelt, entertaining, and always completely honest.

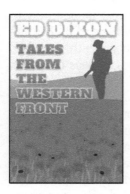

Tales from the Western Front

By Ed Dixon

Tales from the Western Front is a collection of stories about the people and places encountered by the author during more than three decades of visiting the battlefields, graveyards, towns and villages of France and Belgium.

Characters tragic and comic, famous and humble live within these pages, each connected by the common thread of the Great War. Meet Harry Lauder, the great Scottish entertainer and first international superstar; Tommy Armour, golf champion and war hero; "Hoodoo" Kinross, VC, the Pride of Lougheed; the Winslow Boy; Albert Ball, and Jackie the Soldier Baboon among many others.

Each chapter is a story in itself and fully illustrated with photos past and present.

For details of new and forthcoming books
from Extremis Publishing,
please visit our official website at:

www.extremispublishing.com

or follow us on social media at:

www.facebook.com/extremispublishing

www.linkedin.com/company/extremis-publishing-ltd-/

Lightning Source UK Ltd.
Milton Keynes UK
UKHW011816051218
333510UK00010B/248/P